GOLD
experience
2ND EDITION

WORKBOOK

A1
Pre-Key for Schools

CONTENTS

Listening	Speaking	Writing	Review
topic: homes **task:** multiple choice (pictures)	**topic:** phone conversations **task:** making a phone call	**topic:** favourite things **task:** write about your favourite things	unit check 1
topic: 'walk to school' month **task:** gap fill	**topic:** a school timetable **task:** talking about your school day	**topic:** school **task:** write interview questions	unit check 2 review: units 1–2 (p24)
topic: a visit to the Peru cloud forest **task:** matching	**topic:** similarities and differences between animals **task:** talking about animals	**topic:** amazing animals **task:** write a description of an animal	unit check 3
topic: finding things in a picture **task:** colouring and writing	**topic:** visiting a new place **task:** asking for help	**topic:** notes, lists and messages **task:** write a message	unit check 4 review: units 1–4 (p42)
topic: a music festival **task:** matching	**topic:** picture pairs **task:** finding differences between two pictures	**topic:** planning a party **task:** write a description of a party	unit check 5
topic: the Jorvik Viking Centre **task:** multiple choice (pictures)	**topic:** history projects and quizzes **task:** supporting a partner	**topic:** a visit to an interesting place **task:** write a blog post	unit check 6 review: units 1–6 (p60)
topic: building a toy brick tower **task:** gap fill	**topic:** holidays (picture stories) **task:** telling a story from pictures	**topic:** celebrities **task:** write about a famous person	unit check 7
topic: world records and clothes **task:** gap fill	**topic:** world records and places **task:** making guesses about pictures	**topic:** twins at school **task:** write a short story	unit check 8 review: units 1–8 (p78)
topic: free time activities **task:** multiple choice (short texts)	**topic:** talking about plans **task:** planning an activity weekend	**topic:** holiday activities **task:** write a postcard	unit check 9 review: units 1–9 (p88)
topic: a video diary **task:** multiple choice (long text)	**topic:** different types of film **task:** giving opinions	**topic:** entertainment **task:** write a review	

Starter   Welcome to my world

1 Choose the correct answer, A, B or C.

1 A: Hello! Are you new at this school?
   B: A Yes, I do.   **B** Yes, it is.   **C** Yes, I am.

2 A: My name's Daisy. What's your name?
   B: A My name's Paul.   **B** That's Paul.   **C** This is Paul.

3 A: How old are you, Paul?
   B: A I've got ten.   **B** I'm ten.   **C** I'm old.

4 A: I like basketball. Do you?
   B: A Not really.   **B** No, thank you. **C** Yes really.

5 A: What's your favourite sport?
   B: A Music.   **B** Football.   **C** Cats.

6 A: My brother likes football. His name's Tom.
   B: A How old is she?   **B** How is he?   **C** How old is he?
   A: He's twelve.

2 Match the figures (A–J) with the numbers.

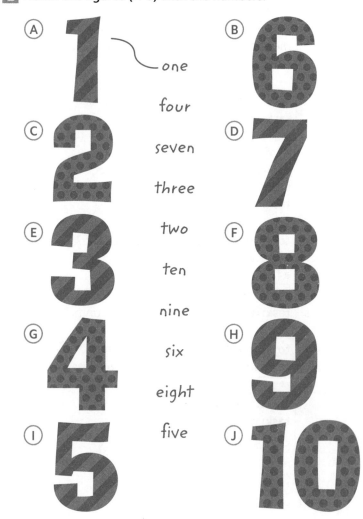

one
four
seven
three
two
ten
nine
six
eight
five

3 Read the clues and complete the crossword.

Across
1 This is Daisy's favourite sport. It's a ball game.
2 This is Daisy's favourite hobby. She listens to it on the school bus.
3 This is Daisy's favourite animal.
Down
4 This is Daisy's favourite food.
5 This is Daisy's favourite thing at school.
6 This is Daisy's favourite colour.

4 Complete the sentences. Use 's.

Elaine / pictures
They are Elaine's pictures ....

1 Daniel / ruler
   It ....

2 my family / dogs
   They ....

3 my mum / sister
   She ....

4 Josef / books
   They ....

5 my cousin / pen
   It ....

6 my best friend / dad
   He ....

7 Molly / friends
   They ....

8 Sam / favourite colour
   It ....

5 Complete the table with these words.

| aunt | brother | cousin | dad | grandad | grandma |
| grandparent | mother | parent | sister | uncle |

male	female	male or female

6 🔊 S.1 **Listen to Mike talking about his family. Write the family words and ages you hear.**

The Holman family

Lily: grandma   65

Tim: ....

Ellen: ....

Fluffy: ....

Alex: ....

Jenny: ....

Jill: ....

Charlie: ....

7 Complete Mike's sentences with possessive adjectives.

1 .... family name is Holman. We're a big family.

2 .... name's Mike. I'm eleven.

3 This is my grandma. .... name is Lily.

4 This is my cat. .... name is Fluffy.

5 This is my brother. .... name is Alex.

6 Here are my parents. .... names are Tim and Ellen.

7 This is my uncle. .... birthday is next week.

8 Rewrite the sentences about the Holman family.

Lily is a man. Lily isn't a man.

1 Mike's cat isn't very old. ....

2 His parents are from Manchester.

....

3 Mike's aunt isn't forty-one. ....

4 Jill is his uncle. ....

5 Charlie and Jill aren't parents. ....

9 Write the next number.

1 twenty-one, twenty-two, twenty-three, ...

2 thirty-seven, thirty-eight, thirty-nine, ...

3 sixty-three, sixty-five, sixty-seven, ...

4 eighteen, seventeen, sixteen, ...

5 eighty, eighty-two, eighty-four, ...

6 eighty-five, ninety, ninety-five, ...

10 Complete the questions. Then answer for you. Use complete sentences.

1 How old .... you?

....

2 What .... your family name?

....

3 Where .... you from?

....

4 What .... your mum's name?

....

5 How old .... your parents?

....

6 Where .... your grandparents from?

....

1 🔊 S.2 **Listen, speak and record your answers.**

Can you spell 'March?'   M–A–R–C–H.

2 🔊 S.3 **Listen and check your answers.**

3 🔊 S.4 **Listen and complete the form.**

Our pop bio this week is all about the One Direction star!

First name: ......Harry......

Second name: [1] ....

Birthday: [2] ....

Home: [3] ....

Family: sister [4] .... and [5] .... Mike

Name of pop group at school: [6] ....
Eskimo

Favourite football team: [7] .... United

4 **Complete the questions and short answers.**

1 A: .... pop music your favourite?
   B: Yes, ...
2 A: .... you a fan of Harry Styles?
   B: No, ...
3 A: .... Harry a good singer?
   B: Yes, ...
4 A: .... Gemma Harry's sister?
   B: Yes, ...
5 A: .... Harry's parents from the USA?
   B: No, ...
6 A: .... Harry's birthday in February?
   B: Yes, ...
7 A: .... Liverpool Harry's favourite team?
   B: No, ...

5 **Write the dates.**

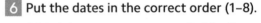

	01/02	1st February
1	24/12	....
2	03/09	....
3	27/10	....
4	10/08	....
5	05/11	....

6 **Put the dates in the correct order (1–8).**

14th July	....	3rd April	....
15th May	....	4th July	....
10th June	....	26th January	....
2nd January	....	12th March	....

7 Put the letters in the correct order to make countries.

insap   Sp a i n

1 eth sau   T_ _   _ _ _

2 tkyure   T_ _ _ _ _

3 dplano   P_ _ _ _ _

4 tiiarbn   B_ _ _ _ _ _

5 saliautra   A_ _ _ _ _ _ _ _

8 Write the nationalities in the correct group.

~~Australia~~   Brazil   Britain   China   Poland   Russia   Spain

-an	-ish	-ese
Australian		

9 Rewrite the sentences.

The man is from Russia.

He is Russian .

1 The girl is from China.

She .

2 The children are from Spain.

They .

3 The car is from Britain.

It .

She's Turkish.

She is from Turkey .

4 They're Mexican.

They .

5 He's Brazilian.

He .

6 The hat is American.

It .

10 Read about Ala and Luke. Match 1–6 with A–F to make sentences.

Hi! I'm Ala Nawrocka and I'm from Poland. I'm eleven years old. My brother's name is Victor. He's sixteen. This is a photo of us. My cousin, Martyn, is here too.

Hi, Ala! Nice to meet you! My name's Luke and I'm twelve. I'm from Britain. This is a photo of me and my two sisters, Ruby and Hayley. They're fifteen. They're twins!

1 Ala   **A** is Ala's cousin.

2 Hayley and Ruby   **B** is from Britain.

3 Ruby   **C** is Ala's brother.

4 Martyn   **D** are Luke's sisters.

5 Luke   **E** is eleven.

6 Victor   **F** is fifteen years old.

11 Read about Ala and Luke again. Write short answers.

1 Is Ala from Poland? ....

2 Is Victor Ala's cousin? ....

3 Is Victor sixteen? ....

4 Is Luke Polish? ....

5 Are Ruby and Haley twins? ....

6 Are Ruby and Hayley twelve? ....

1 Come in

VOCABULARY 1

things in a room

1 Label the picture with these words.

chair   clock   curtains
~~desk~~   laptop   shelf   wardrobe

2 What other things can you see in the picture? Complete the words.

1 g u _ _ _ _   **4** b a _
2 p o _ _ _ _   **5** b o _ _
3 b i _

3 Write the words in the correct group.

bed covers   clock   cushion   lamp
laptop   mat   mirror
noticeboard   pictures   shelf   TV

electrical	on the wall	material

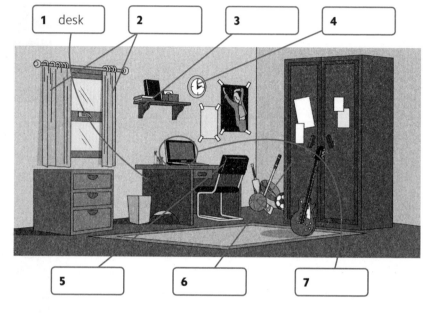

1 desk	2	3	4

5	6	7

prepositions of place

4 Look at the pictures. Complete the sentences.

①   ②    ③

④    ⑤    ⑥

1 The comic is .... the bin.
2 The mouse is .... the cupboard.
3 The mobile phone is .... the desk.
4 The clock is .... the shelf.
5 The cat is .... the TV.
6 The mirror is .... the cupboard.

READING

1 Read the story and answer the questions.

1 Who is Max?

....

2 Where is the box?

....

3 How many doors are there in the room?

....

2 **e** Read the story again. Complete the sentences with one, two or three words in each gap.

Picture A

The green bedroom is Ana's ....favourite.... room.

1 Isobel wants to look inside the ....

Picture B

2 The pictures .... the table.

3 The pictures are from ....

4 There isn't a .... in the room.

Picture C

5 There are .... the room.

6 The .... is behind the curtain.

3 Do you have a favourite room in your house? What is it? Why do you like it?

....

....

....

4 Read the story again. How is this room different from your bedroom at home? Write 25 words. Use the vocabulary and prepositions to help you.

In my bedroom there aren't pictures. There is a bin next to my desk ...

A special room

Isobel and her brother, Max, are in a very old house today. Ana works here. She's telling them all about one of the bedrooms.

'Welcome to the green bedroom. It's my favourite room in the house. Look at the bed. There are curtains! These curtains are from France,' Ana says.
'Look!' Isobel says. 'Next to the bed, there's a big box. Can I look inside it?'

'Look! There are five pictures on the wall above the table. They are all from Britain. And there's a beautiful clock. It's 200 years old.
But is there a bin in the room? No, there isn't.

'Now, how many doors are there in this room? Look around ... One ... two ... surprise! There are three doors. There's a secret door behind this curtain.'

GRAMMAR

there is/there are (+ some/any)

1 Match 1–6 with A–F to make sentences.

1	Are there any	**A**	Italian book.
2	There are some books	**B**	on the shelf.
3	There aren't any	**C**	a cupboard.
4	There's	**D**	messages in the bin?
5	There isn't an	**E**	curtains.
6	There isn't a	**F**	desk next to the bed.

2 Look at the photo of the room and answer the questions. Use *Yes, there is/are* or *No, there isn't/aren't*.

1 Is there a bin? ....

2 Are there any posters? ....

3 Is there a guitar? ....

4 Are there any lamps? ....

5 Is there a laptop? ....

6 Are there any curtains? ....

3 Make questions. Use *Is there / Are there* and *your*.

pictures / bedroom

Are there any pictures in your bedroom? ....

1 pencil case / bag

....

2 books / shelves

....

3 clock / bedroom

....

4 mobile phone / bag

....

5 computer games / desk

....

4 Answer the questions in Ex 3.

1 ....

2 ....

3 ....

4 ....

5 ....

5 Look at the picture. Complete the text with these words.

a	any	are	aren't	's	isn't	some

There **¹**........................... a school bag on the table. It's my bag! What's in my bag? There's **²**........................... banana for my snack. There **³**........................... a drink. There aren't **⁴**........................... pencils, but there are **⁵**........................... pens. There **⁶**........................... notebooks for my school work. And, of course, there's my mobile phone! There **⁷**........................... any pictures on it at the moment.

VOCABULARY 2

the home

1 Look at the photos and choose the correct words.

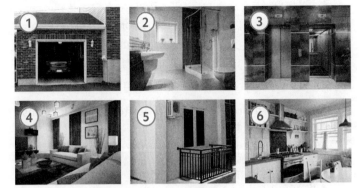

1 kitchen / bathroom /(garage)
2 bathroom / kitchen / balcony
3 garden / lift / balcony
4 living room / bathroom / bedroom
5 lift / balcony / dining room
6 garden / stairs / kitchen

2 Read the sentences and label the picture with these names. There is one person in each room.

~~Ben~~   Ben's cat   Dad   Grandma   Jenny   Mum

Ben is in the garden.
1 There's a man in the bathroom.
2 The woman in the kitchen isn't Ben's mum or his sister.
3 There's a pet on the stairs.
4 Ben's sister is called Jenny. She's downstairs.
5 Ben's mum is upstairs.

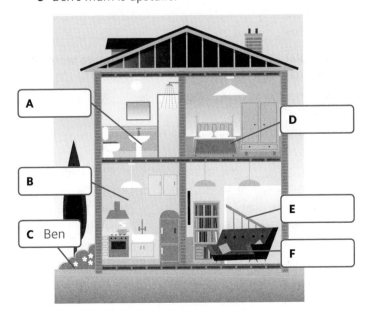

3 Decide if the words are inside (I), outside(O) or both (B).

kitchen	...I...	**4**	garage	....
1 lift	....	**5**	balcony	....
2 bedroom	....	**6**	stairs	....
3 garden	....	**7**	bathroom	....

4 **e** Look at the picture and follow the instructions.

Sunday morning

Complete the sentences.

1 There are two children upstairs, in the ....
2 A car is in ....

Answer the questions.

3 How many pets are downstairs?

....

4 Where is the man?

....

Write two sentences about the picture.

5 ....

....

6 ....

....

11

LISTENING

1 🔊 **1.1 Listen to two children and their mum talking about homes. Answer the questions.**

1 Have the family got a house or an apartment now?
....

2 Has it got a garden? ....

3 What pet have they got? ....

4 How many bedrooms have they got now?
....

5 Is the new house near the school? ....

6 When can they see the new house? ....

2 e 🔊 **1.2 Listen again and choose the correct answer, A, B or C.**

1 Which is the family's home?

 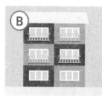 

2 Which is the family's balcony?

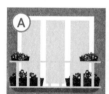  

3 Which is the boy's bedroom?

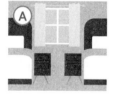 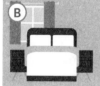 

4 Where is the house?

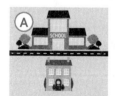  

5 Who does Mum need to call?

have got

3 Complete the sentences with *have* or *has*.

1 Angela .... got lots of books in her bedroom.

2 My house .... got stairs.

3 The cat .... got a cushion in the kitchen.

4 We .... got six chairs in the living room.

5 I .... got a new mobile phone.

6 My parents .... got a big bed.

4 Put the words in the correct order to make questions. Then complete the answers.

your / a / flat / has / got / balcony?

A: Has your flat got a balcony? ....

B: Yes, it has ....

1 your / garden / house / got / has / a?
A: ....
B: No, ...

2 have / house / got / stairs / you / your / in?
A: ....
B: Yes, ...

3 a / pet / got / you / have?
A: ....
B: No, ...

4 apartment / your / lift / has / got / a?
A: ....
B: Yes, ...

5 have / a / garage / you / your / apartment / got / under?
A: ....
B: No , ...

6 your / has / got / sister / room / a / big?
A: ....
B: Yes, ...

5 Complete the conversation with one or two words in each gap. Use short forms where possible.

A: Good morning, Eve. You ......'ve...... got a fantastic house!

B: Thank you. It's an old windmill.

A: How many rooms **1**.......................... it got?

B: **2**.......................... got seven rooms. One of the bedrooms is downstairs and it's **3**.......................... a living room upstairs.

A: And how many stairs **4**.......................... your house got?

B: I don't know! I think **5**.......................... got fifty.

A: Have **6**.......................... got a big bedroom?

B: No, I **7**.......................... . My bedroom is round and it's got small windows, but I love it!

SPEAKING

1 🔊 **1.3 Listen and repeat.**

1	Alice:	02079 460 395
2	Emma:	01614 960 712
3	John:	02920 180 438
4	Karen:	08081 570 864
5	Pete:	03069 990 357
6	Susan:	07700 900 156

2 🔊 **1.4 Listen, speak and record.**

3 🔊 **1.5 Listen back and compare.**

4 🔊 **1.6 Listen and write the mobile numbers.**

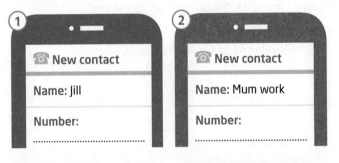

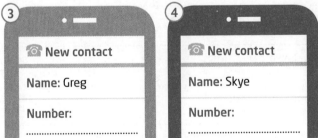

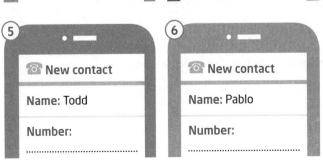

5 Choose the correct answer, A, B or C.

1 **A:** Hello?
  B: A OK.
  B Hello, Mr Bull.
  C Bye.

2 **A:** Hi, Peter!
  B: A Is there Ethan?
  B Where's Ethan?
  C Is Ethan there, please?

3 **A:** Yes, he is. Just a minute.
  B: A Hi.
  B Thank you.
  C That's OK.

4 **A:** Hi, Peter. Are you OK?
  B: A Yes, thanks.
  B OK.
  C No, thanks.

5 **A:** What date is your party again?
  B: A At five o'clock.
  B The tenth of October.
  C I don't know.

6 **A:** Great, thanks. Bye for now!
  B: A Good afternoon.
  B Hi.
  C Bye.

6 Write the phrases in the correct group. Write one phrase from each pair in each group.

Are you OK? / How are you?   Bye. / Goodbye.   Hello. / Hi.
No problem. / Of course.   Thanks. / Thank you.

☎ **family, friends and children**

☎ **other people**

WRITING

1 Rewrite the sentences with the correct punctuation.

today is tuesday 14 february
Today is Tuesday 14 February.

1 this is me in london in september

....

2 my friend will is australian

....

3 this is my chinese friend, mai

....

4 the party is on saturday 10 march

....

5 we've got a holiday house in malaga, spain

....

2 Choose the correct words to complete the sentences.

1 This is a photo **of** / **about** my dog.
2 This is a postcard **of** / **from** my cousin.
3 This is a menu **from** / **about** my favourite café.
4 It's a film **of** / **about** a big house.
5 It's a ticket **for** / **of** a concert.
6 Is this a birthday **board** / **card**?

3 Look at the pictures from Maria's bedroom wall. Match the pictures (A–C) with the sentences (1–3).

1 This is a photo of my brother. ....
2 This is a postcard from my uncle in Paris. ....
3 Here's a concert ticket. My favourite music is rock. ....

4 Read the project and answer the questions.

The Beatles
London Palladium
13 October

A family photo

by Elena

This is a photo of my grandparents in 1963. Their names are Mary and Edward Forest. In the photo they're in London, on holiday. They live in Birmingham now. The ticket is for a concert in London. My grandparents still love the Beatles today!

1 Who are the people in the photo?

....

2 What's their family name?

....

3 Where are they in the photo?

....

4 What's the ticket for?

....

5 What's the date of the concert?

....

6 What's the name of the group playing at the concert?

....

5 Draw a picture of a family or find a real photo. Draw a ticket, menu or postcard for the picture. Write about:

• who the people are.
• where they are.
• what the ticket/menu/postcard is.

UNIT CHECK

1 Look at the picture. Put the letters in the correct order to make words.

1 rissta ....
2 preost ....
3 colkc ....
4 fitl ....
5 brtneiooacd ....
6 hirac ....

2 Look at the picture again. Choose the correct words to complete the sentences.

1 There's a clock **under** / **on** the wall.
2 There's a poster **between** / **behind** the cupboard and the noticeboard.
3 There isn't a mat **on** / **in** the floor.
4 The stairs are **behind** / **above** the wall.
5 One of the men is **in front of** / **between** the lift.
6 There's a noticeboard **above** / **next to** the chair.

3 Complete the sentences about the picture with one word in each gap.

There ...... isn't ...... a bin in the picture.

1 There .... a clock between the lift and the poster.
2 There .... three men in the picture.
3 There .... any windows in the picture.
4 There .... a cushion on the chair.
5 There are .... messages on the noticeboard.

4 Choose the correct answer, A, B or C.

1 I like cooking. The ...... is my favourite room.
   A bathroom   B kitchen   C balcony
2 There's a ...... next to my house. My dad's car is there.
   A bin   B lift   C garage
3 I'm from Spain. There's a ...... outside my apartment.
   A balcony   B bedroom   C stairs
4 I've got a swimming pool in my ....
   A bedroom   B garden   C kitchen
5 There are two ...... in my house – one upstairs and one downstairs.
   A stairs   B bathrooms   C downstairs
6 There is a big ...... in our house, with a table and ten chairs.
   A dining room   B bathroom   C garage
7 I've got a ...... in my bedroom so I can do my homework.
   A shelf   B mirror   C desk

5 Complete the conversation with these words.

'--

's any got has hasn't haven't It's

'--

A: Hello! Welcome to my house.
B: Thank you. You **1** .... got a lovely home. Which is your favourite room?
A: The living room. It **2** .... got four windows and all my posters on the walls.
B: Sorry, but I think your house **3** .... got stairs. Is that true?
A: No, it hasn't got **4** .... stairs. There's a special lift.
B: Wow! And how many bedrooms has the house **5** .... ?
A: **6** .... got ten bedrooms.
B: Have you got a big family?
A: No, I **7** .... I've got lots of pets.

2 What a week!

VOCABULARY 1

everyday activities

1 Put the days of the week in the correct order (1–7).

Friday	....
Monday	....
Saturday	....
Sunday	....
Thursday	....
Tuesday	....
Wednesday	....

2 Match 1–7 with A–G to make phrases.

1	have	**A**	dressed
2	have	**B**	to bed
3	get	**C**	breakfast
4	go to	**D**	shower
5	have a	**E**	dinner
6	watch	**F**	school
7	go	**G**	TV

3 What do you do on a school day? Put the sentences in the correct order (1–8).

I go to school.	....
I have breakfast.	....
I go home.	....
I get up at seven.	__1__
I do my homework.	....
I go to bed.	....
I get dressed.	....
I have dinner.	....

4 Complete the text with these words.

do   get   go   have   meet   play

Saturday is my favourite day of the week. It's so different from a school day.
I **1**........................ up at 9.30! In the morning
I **2**........................ my friends in town.
I **3**........................ lunch with my parents in a restaurant. My friends and I **4**........................ to my house and **5**........................ computer games in the afternoon. After my friends go home, I **6**........................ my homework and watch TV.

5 What do you do on Saturday? Write five sentences about your activities.

....
....
....
....
....

READING

1 Read the article quickly. Match the questions (1–5) with the answers (A–E).

1 Where does the teacher work? ....
2 How old are the students? ....
3 How many hours of school are there in a day? ....
4 How many hours of school are there in a week? ....
5 Where is the classroom? ....

A fifteen
B three
C in a dining room
D between nine and fourteen
E in a theatre

2 e Read the article again. Choose the correct answer for each gap.

	A	**B**	**C**
1	am	is	are
2	because	for	and
3	in	of	for
4	do	go	have
5	at	to	when

3 Read the article again. Complete the students' timetable.

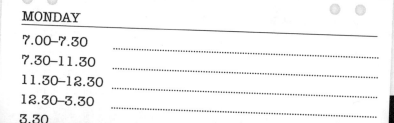

MONDAY
7.00–7.30 ....
7.30–11.30 ....
11.30–12.30 ....
12.30–3.30 ....
3.30 ....

Teacher profile
Angela Barns

Our teacher this week is Angela Barns. She **¹**....... a teacher but she doesn't work in a school.

'I teach young actors in the theatre in London. My job is called tutoring.

I work with children aged between nine and fourteen. They are all actors **²**....... they are students, too! This week I have two children. They don't work before seven **³**....... the morning or after seven in the evening.

The children don't have a regular school day. It starts at seven o'clock, when they get up and **⁴**....... breakfast. They come to the theatre at 7.30 and work for four hours, then they have lunch. Then they study with me for three hours in the afternoon. They do their homework in the evening or in their breaks. Some child actors have extra lessons on Saturdays or Sundays.

I don't teach the children in a classroom. We use the dining room at the theatre.

Working as a tutor is very different from working in a normal school. I don't see other teachers and my day doesn't finish **⁵**....... 3.30 like the students. But I love my job!'

GRAMMAR

present simple: positive and negative

1 Write true sentences about you.

meet friends on Saturday

I meet / I don't meet my friends on Saturday.

1 get up at 8.00 on Sunday

....

2 have breakfast with my parents

....

3 go to bed at 9.00 in the evening

....

4 play computer games in my bedroom

....

5 watch TV in the morning

....

2 Choose the correct words to complete the text.

Life at St Edmund's **Music School**

School subjects

St Edmund's is a music school, but the children **¹studies / study** regular subjects too. The school also **²has / have** after school clubs for art and computing.

The school day

Students at the school **³gets / get** up at 6.30 in the morning. Music lessons **⁴starts / start** at 7.30. After 11.00 there are different classes. Lunch is at 12.30. The school day **⁵finish / finishes** at 5.00 in the afternoon.

The school week

There are no music lessons on Saturday. The school **⁶don't / doesn't** open on Sunday.

3 Clara is a student at St Edmund's Music School. Write what she does at these times.

1 6.30 in the morning

She ....

2 12.30

She ....

3 7.30

She ....

4 Saturday

She ....

4 Complete the text. Use the present simple form of the verbs in brackets.

On Sunday I ......*get up*...... (get up) at 8.00. I have breakfast and play computer games with my little sister. She **¹**.......................... (love) computer games. Then I meet my cousins. We **²**.......................... (not meet) at their house – we meet in the park. We play some sport and then we **³**.......................... (go) to my house and **⁴**.......................... (have) lunch. My dad cooks all week but he **⁵**.......................... (not cook) on Sunday. It's mum's turn! In the afternoon my cousins **⁶**.......................... (go) home and I do my homework.

5 Read the text in Ex 4 again and put the pictures (A–D) in the correct order (1–4).

VOCABULARY 2

free time activities

1 Label the photos with these words.

have swimming   play card games   the guitar   volleyball

1 play ....

2 .... lessons

3 play ....

4 ....

2 Read the sentences and complete the table with the free time verbs and activities.

- Mary has singing lessons the day after she plays the guitar.
- The girls play the guitar together.
- Anne goes to the cinema on Sunday.
- One boy and one girl go to the beach at the weekend.
- One child plays computer games on Sunday.
- Ben doesn't play computer games.
- The girls don't play computer games or volleyball.
- Ben plays volleyball on Monday.
- Rob plays football the day after his swimming lesson.

	Sunday	Monday	Tuesday
Ben	go to the beach	**1**	have piano lessons
Rob	**2**	**3**	**4** ....
Mary	**5**	play the guitar	**6** ....
Anne	**7**	**8**	play football

3 Complete the text with *play*, *have* or *go*.

This is a photo of me and my brother. We're from Australia and we love living here. Every day after school we **1** .... to the beach. Children here don't **2** .... swimming lessons in a pool – we learn to swim in the sea. We also **3** .... volleyball on the beach and we like to **4** .... card games when it's too hot. In the evening we **5** .... to the cinema or **6** .... computer games.

4 Choose the correct words to complete the sentences.

1 Ella goes to the cinema in **Saturday / the evening / night**.
2 She has guitar lessons on **Wednesday / the afternoon / five o'clock**.
3 The lessons start at **the morning / nine o'clock / time**.
4 She goes on holiday with her family in **Sunday / August / tomorrow**.
5 Her birthday is in **tomorrow / Tuesday / May**.
6 It's on 16 **May / Friday / tomorrow**.

5 Complete the sentences with *in*, *on* or *at*.

1 I go to school from Monday to Friday and .... Saturday morning.
2 I don't go to school .... Sunday.
3 We have holidays .... July and August.
4 After school I get home .... four o'clock.
5 I play football .... the afternoon and then I watch TV.
6 I do my homework .... the weekend.

LISTENING

1 **Look at the photo and guess.**

1 Where are the children?

....

2 Who is the woman?

....

2 🔊 **2.1 Listen. Are the sentences true (T) or false (F)?**

1 Dillon has got a badge for playing football. ....

2 He meets the walking group in the park. ....

3 They get a badge every week. ....

4 Mrs Greenhow is Dillon's teacher. ....

5 Dillon's dad goes to work by train. ....

6 Rob's school starts in ten minutes. ....

3 e 🔊 **2.2 Listen again. Complete the advert.**

WALK TO SCHOOL MONTH

1 'Walk to School' month is in ....

2 The walking group meets at .... o'clock.

3 The leader of the group is Mrs ....

4 Parents can walk with the children on .... morning.

5 This month's picture on the badge is a ....

present simple: questions and short answers

4 **Choose the correct words to complete the sentences.**

1 **Do / Does** your big brother go to your school?

2 What time **do / does** you get up in the morning?

3 **Do / Does** your sister have swimming lessons?

4 What time **do / does** your guitar lesson start?

5 **Do / Does** your parents help you with your homework?

6 What time **do / does** the school bus leave?

5 **Match the questions (1–6) with the answers (A–F).**

1 Do you play football? ....

2 Do your parents go to the cinema? ....

3 Do you have a brother? ....

4 Do you have piano lessons? ....

5 Does your dad play computer games? ....

6 Do your friends play volleyball? ....

A No, I don't. I play the guitar.

B Yes, they do. They play after school.

C No, he doesn't. He watches TV.

D Yes, I do. His name is Pedro.

E Yes, they do. They like films.

F Yes, I do. I love sport.

6 **Briony is a child actor. Complete the questions about her job. Use *do/does* and these words.**

get up	have	like	meet	teach	work

1 .... you .... at the weekend?

2 .... you .... early in the morning?

3 .... your tutor .... you on Sunday?

4 .... your friends .... you at the theatre?

5 .... you .... singing lessons?

6 .... your mum .... meeting famous actors?

SPEAKING

1 🔊 2.3 **Look, listen and repeat.**

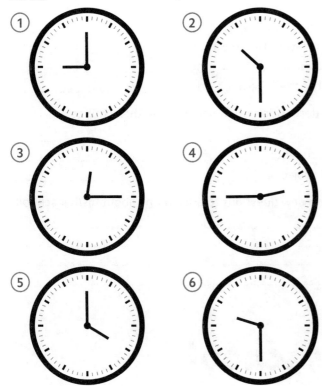

2 🔊 2.4 **Listen, speak and record.**

3 🔊 2.5 **Listen back and compare.**

4 **Look at the clocks in Ex 1 and write the times. Use words, not numbers.**

1 School starts at <u>nine o'clock</u> .
2 We have morning break at .
3 We have lunch at .
4 We have afternoon break at .
5 School finishes at .
6 I go to bed at .

5 **Make the sentences in Ex 4 true for you.**

1
2
3
4
5
6

6 **Talk about your timetable in Ex 5. Record yourself. Listen to your recording. What can you improve?**

7 **Complete the conversation with one word in each gap.**

A: Come on, Dad! It's eight fifteen.

B: What ¹................ does school start?

A: Dad! It ²................ at eight forty-five. Let's go!

B: Where's your sports bag? ³................ you have sport today?

A: No, I ⁴................ . Sport is on Friday, ⁵................ the afternoon.

B: OK. But you have football after school today.

A: No, I don't. It's Tuesday. I ⁶................ a guitar lesson today.

B: Oh yes. Where's your guitar?

A: I've got it. Let's go!

8 🔊 2.6 **Listen and complete Harry's timetable.**

	MONDAY	TUESDAY
¹ .....9.00.....	maths	English
²	break	
11.00	⁵	geography
³	lunch	
1.30	history	music
⁴	break	
3.00	art	⁶ ....

WRITING

1 Rewrite the sentences with apostrophes.

1 My name is Elisa.

....

2 I have got a little sister.

....

3 We are both at the same school.

....

4 Elisa does not like school.

....

5 She has got a pet rabbit.

....

6 It is called Fluffy.

....

2 You are writing an email to a new friend. Complete the questions to find out the same information.

I'm twelve. How <u>old are you</u> .... ?

1 I've got one brother and one sister. Have .... ?

2 My school day starts at 9.00. What .... ?

3 History is my favourite subject. What's .... ?

4 I like playing basketball. Which sport .... ?

5 I go to the beach at the weekend. What .... ?

3 Read Oliver's description of his school. Find these things.

1 name of the school: ....

2 number of students: ....

3 four school subjects: ....

4 Write four interview questions to ask a friend about his/her school.

....

....

....

....

My school

My school is called Ashwood High. It's in Grantby and it's got around 500 students.

The school day starts at 8.45 and it finishes at 3.30. We have lessons from Monday to Friday, but not at the weekend. I love school. I like geography and English, but I don't like maths.

My favourite place in the school is the theatre. We have drama lessons there on Friday afternoon. Drama is fun, but learning lines is difficult!

UNIT CHECK

1 Write the word that comes before each group.

1	a shower	a lesson	fun
2	to bed	to the beach	to school
3	the morning	the afternoon	the evening
4	card games	the guitar	football
5	breakfast	a party	singing lessons
6	my birthday	Monday	12 July

2 Look at the timetable. Complete the text with one word in each gap.

Monday	Tuesday	Wednesday
🎨	X + Y △	✒️
🎨	⚗️	✒️
Lunch	**Lunch**	**Lunch**
🌐	🏉🪖	X + Y △
X ÷ Y △	✒️📖	X + Y △

Here's my school ...*timetable*... . On Monday morning
I have two ¹.......................... lessons. Lunch is at 12.30.
After lunch I have ².......................... and maths. On Tuesday
morning I have maths, then ³.......................... . That's
my favourite ⁴.......................... . In the afternoon I have
⁵.......................... and English. On Wednesdays I have
English and maths.
I don't like Wednesday afternoons!

3 Choose the correct answer, A, B or C.

1 Does your father have swimming lessons?

A No, she doesn't. **B** No, we don't. **C** No, he doesn't.

2 What time do you have your English lessons?

A At 10.00. **B** Yes, I do. **C** No, they don't.

3 Do you and your friends go to the beach at the weekend?

A Yes, they do. **B** Yes, I do. **C** Yes, we do.

4 Do you like science?

A No, he doesn't. **B** No, I don't. **C** No, it doesn't.

5 Does your sister play the guitar?

A Yes, she does. **B** Yes, he does. **C** Yes, they do.

6 When do you go to bed?

A In the morning. **B** In March. **C** At nine o'clock.

4 Complete the sentences with the present simple form of the verbs in brackets.

1 School .... (not start) at eight o'clock in Britain.

2 I .... (not have) lunch at school.

3 We .... (not play) the drums early in the morning.

4 My teacher .... (not like) people talking in class.

5 My cousin .... (not go) to my school.

6 Those girls .... (not travel) on my bus.

5 Look at the pictures. Complete the sentences. Use the times on the clocks.

1 I get up at .... My sister Jo gets up at ....

2 I have breakfast at .... Jo has breakfast at ....

3 We go to school at ....

4 I do my homework at .... Jo does her homework at ....

5 We watch TV at ....

REVIEW: UNITS 1–2

1 Choose the correct answer, A, B or C.

1 What's your name?
  A Why?
  B I'm thirteen.
  C Harry.

2 How old are you?
  A I'm twelve.
  B I'm OK.
  C She's twelve.

3 What's your family name?
  A Three.
  B Martinez.
  C I don't know.

4 Are you from Brazil?
  A No, you aren't.
  B No, I'm not.
  C No, it isn't.

5 Have you got a brother or sister?
  A Yes, I've got a brother.
  B No, I have.
  C Yes, I am.

6 Is there a clock in your room?
  A No, I haven't.
  B Yes, I am.
  C Yes, there is.

2 Put the words in the correct order to make sentences.

1 colour / my / favourite / red / is

....

2 number / our / is / house / forty-three

....

3 bedroom / covers / in / bed / my / the / blue / are

....

4 are / door / the / keys / where?

....

5 room / pictures / are / any / your / in / there / living?

....

6 have / you / phone / Charlie's / number / got / mobile?

....

7 house / in / bedrooms / are / there / three / our

....

8 walls / got / has / my / yellow / room

....

3 Complete Simon's post with one word in each gap.

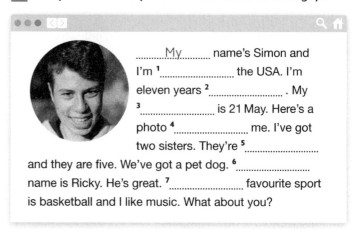

...........My........... name's Simon and I'm **1**........................ the USA. I'm eleven years **2**........................ . My **3**........................ is 21 May. Here's a photo **4**........................ me. I've got two sisters. They're **5**........................ and they are five. We've got a pet dog. **6**........................ name is Ricky. He's great. **7**........................ favourite sport is basketball and I like music. What about you?

4 Match the people (1–6) with the pets (A–F). Make sentences.

Georgina / Britain   Tom / the USA   Carmen / Spain

Yuri / Russia   Natalia / Brazil   Metin / Turkey

 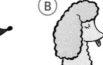

1 _F_ Georgina's cats are British.
2 ....
3 ....
4 ....
5 ....
6 ....

5 Look at the picture of Charlie's room. Complete the sentences.

1 There's a .... and a .... on the desk.

2 There's a .... on the wall.

3 There are two .... on the bed.

4 The .... are in front of the window. They're white.

5 Look at the shoes on the floor. Charlie likes ....

6 Make negative sentences. Use the present simple.

1 I / play / the drums

....

2 my dad / play / card games

....

3 there / be / clock / our living room

....

4 there / be / pictures / their kitchen

....

5 we / have got / dining room / our house

....

6 Silvia / have got / desk / her bedroom

....

7 Complete the questions about Jenny.

1 A: Where .... ?

B: The USA.

2 A: What is her .... ?

B: Williams.

3 A: How .... ?

B: She's thirty-one.

4 A: What .... teach?

B: She teaches English.

5 A: Does .... the guitar?

B: Yes, she does.

6 A: What .... food?

B: Pizza!

8 e Complete the email with one word in each gap.

Hi Mum,

Today ....is........ my third day at the new job. The school is big – there **1** .... 600 students. I've **2** .... four lessons today, and after school I teach a Spanish **3** ....

School **4** .... at 8.30, but it's near **5** .... house, so I **6** .... travel by car. I walk there **7** .... 7.45.

How is your holiday? Send me a photo **8** .... the beach, please.

See you **9** .... Sunday!

Love,
Jenny

3 Animal magic

VOCABULARY 1

animals

1 Look at the photos and choose the correct words.

kangaroo / bat

duck / dolphin

horse / bear

sheep / shark

whale / bird

mouse / lion

animal actions

2 Look at the animals in Ex 1. What actions can they do? Tick the correct boxes.

	fly	walk	swim	jump	climb	run
1						
2						
3						
4						
5						
6						

3 Complete the sentences with these verbs.

climb   fly   jump   swim   walk

1 Pandas .... trees.
2 Hippos .... in water. They live in Africa.
3 Monkeys climb and .... between trees.
4 Parrots .... and walk.
5 Penguins are birds, but they don't fly. They .... and swim.

4 Think of one more animal. Describe it in 25 words.

....
....
....
....
....

READING

1 Read the post. Find these things.

1 four animals: ....
2 Ellen's favourite month: ....
3 the name of Ellen's hobby: ....

● ● ● ◁ ▷   🔍 🏠

A POST FROM **SCOTLAND**

I live on a farm in Scotland with my **¹**........................... and our
dog, Tweed. My dad always says that Tweed isn't a pet.
He's a working dog. He gets up early in the **²**...........................
and goes out with my dad before breakfast. Tweed helps
with the sheep, goats and pigs. But I think he's my pet
too, because he usually plays with me when I finish
³........................... and he sleeps in my bedroom.

April is my favourite time on the farm. The **⁴**...........................
are with their babies in the field near our house. The babies
usually stay with their mothers for eight weeks. I love
watching them run and jump. They look very funny.

Tweed isn't always at work with the animals. We've got
an interesting hobby – we go to agility competitions. At
agility competitions dogs **⁵**........................... and jump over
special obstacles. Tweed can run very fast, but he doesn't
always **⁶**........................... to me. He sometimes runs under an
obstacle and that means we never win the first prize. But
we love the competitions.

Ellen, *12*, *Aviemore*, *Scotland*

---

2 **e** Read the post again. Choose a word from below.
Write the correct words next to numbers 1–6.

family   house   night

morning   listen   run

school   cats   sheep

3 Choose the best title for the post.

1 A year on a farm
2 Me and my dog
3 All about sheep

Tweed going over an obstacle
at an agility competition

One of our sheep on the farm

GRAMMAR

adverbs of frequency

1 Read the article. Choose the correct answer for each gap.

> Wild kangaroos ¹...... live in Australia. They usually ²...... in groups of about ten. A group of kangaroos is called a mob. They aren't ³...... brown. Some kangaroos are grey. Kangaroos always eat plants. They ⁴...... eat spiders or beetles. Kangaroos aren't usually dangerous, but they ⁵...... attack people. Cars are dangerous for kangaroos. In Australia, there ⁶...... often 'kangaroo crossing' signs next to the roads.

1 A always	**B** aren't	**C** doesn't
2 A have	**B** live	**C** talk
3 A never	**B** always	**C** sometimes
4 A never	**B** always	**C** sometimes
5 A always	**B** sometimes	**C** often
6 A have	**B** do	**C** are

2 Put the words in the correct order to make sentences.

1 milk / has / my cat / never / breakfast / for

....

2 at / goes out / he / night / often

....

3 eat / he / always / food / his / doesn't

....

4 usually / on / sister's / bed / he / sleeps / my

....

5 very / usually / happy / he / is

....

6 in / always / the / the / he / sits / TV / afternoon / in front of

....

3 Complete the post with these words.

are   don't   see   spiders   usually   you

| ABOUT | TRAVEL GUIDE | Q&A | RESTAURANTS | TOP DEALS |

Hi there,

My holiday this year is to Australia. I ¹........................... love visiting a new country, but I am a bit nervous about Australia because of the wild animals. I ²........................... like spiders and I know Australian ones are very big. Can any Australians in the group answer my questions, please?

- ³........................... the spiders in Australia always dangerous?
- Where do ⁴........................... usually see them?
- Do ⁵........................... often come into hotel rooms?
- What do I do when I ⁶........................... a spider?

Thanks, everyone!

Travelbug99

4 Complete the reply to the post in Ex 3. Use the present simple form of the verbs in brackets.

| ABOUT | TRAVEL GUIDE | Q&A | RESTAURANTS | TOP DEALS |

Hi Travelbug99,

I'm sorry that you are nervous about coming to Australia. Please come and visit! Yes, we ¹........................... (see/often) big spiders here! But there are lots of other beautiful animals and birds to see.

The spiders in Australia ²........................... (not be/always) dangerous. Spiders ³........................... (not come/often) out into the open and you ⁴........................... (not see/usually) them in hotel rooms. Here are some things to remember:

- Stay in places with a lot of people. Spiders ⁵........................... (not like/usually) to be with people.
- Never leave your clothes on the floor at night.
- Always look in your shoes before you put them on! Spiders ⁶........................... (climb/sometimes) into people's shoes!
- And ... have fun in Australia!

Ozzieboy

VOCABULARY 2

the world around us

1 Look at the photos and complete the puzzle. Find the mystery word and draw a picture for it.

	¹f	o	r	e	s	t	
	²j				e		
			t				
	³l				e		
	⁴			v		r	
	⁵d		s				

2 Choose the correct words to complete the sentences.

1 Crocodiles usually live in **lakes / deserts**.
2 Fish always live in **water / a cave**.
3 Brown bears usually live in **a river / the mountains**.
4 Camels usually live in the **forest / desert**.
5 Goats never live in the **jungle / mountains**.
6 Sharks never live in **lakes / the sea**.

3 Complete the article with these words.

caves drink fish insects sea the

Bat facts

About bats
Bats are interesting animals. They sleep in the day when ¹_____ sun is up and they come out at night and look for food. Bats don't usually see in colour. They only see in black and white.

Their food
Bats eat lots of different types of food. They often eat ²_____ . A brown bat eats 600 of them in one hour! Some bats also eat ³_____ from lakes or the ⁴_____ . Other bats live in the jungle and they eat fruit and ⁵_____ water from flowers.

Their home
Bats sleep in ⁶_____ or forests. People sometimes make houses for bats in their gardens.

Their babies
Mother bats have one baby a year. Baby bats are called pups. They drink milk from their mother.

4 Make sentences with *usually* or *always*. Use a verb from A and a noun from B.

A ~~eat~~ fly not like sleep swim walk

B caves crocodiles desert forest ~~insects~~ sea

	bats	Bats usually eat insects.
1	parrots	....
2	sharks	....
3	camels	....
4	brown bears	....
5	people	....

LISTENING

1 🔊 **3.1 Look at the brochure. Listen to Laura, Jake and their mum talking about the tour. Answer the questions.**

COME WITH US ON A TOUR OF THE **CLOUD FOREST** IN **PERU!**

QUETZAL IN THE CLOUD FOREST

1 When does the family's tour start? ....
2 What's Laura's favourite bird? ....
3 What animal does Jake love? ....

2 e 🔊 **3.2 Listen again. Which animal (A–F) do people usually see on each day of the tour?**

1 Day 1 ....
2 Day 2 ....
3 Day 3 ....
4 Day 4 ....
5 Day 5 ....
6 Day 6 ....

present simple: question words

3 Match the questions (1–6) with the answers (A–F).

1 Where does the panda live? ....
2 What does it eat? ....
3 When does it sleep? ....
4 Why does it eat all the time? ....
5 How often does it have babies? ....
6 How does it find food? ....

A By walking around.
B Not very often.
C In the mountains.
D Bamboo.
E Because it is a big animal.
F At night.

4 Read the answers and write the questions. Use the highlighted information to choose the question word.

A: How often do lions eat small animals?
B: Lions sometimes eat small animals.

1 **A:** ....
B: Armadillos sleep a lot because they live in hot places.

2 **A:** ....
B: Ducks live near the water.

3 **A:** ....
B: Polar bears never see penguins.

4 **A:** ....
B: Bats sleep in the day.

5 **A:** ....
B: Ducks eat plants, insects and small fish.

SPEAKING

1 🔊 3.3 Listen and repeat.

1 Where does it live?

2 When does it sleep?

3 What does it eat?

4 When does it feed?

5 What does it drink?

6 Has it got legs?

7 Does it climb trees?

8 Does it eat plants?

9 Does it make eggs?

10 Does it have babies?

2 🔊 3.4 Listen, speak and record.

3 🔊 3.5 Listen back and compare.

4 🔊 3.6 Listen and choose the correct answer, A, B or C.

1 A Two years.   **B** In the jungle.   **C** Green and black.

2 A Sometimes.   **B** In the jungle.   **C** Animals and birds.

3 A No, it hasn't.   **B** No, it isn't.   **C** Yes, it has got.

4 A Yes, it has.   **B** Yes, sometimes.   **C** No, it isn't.

5 A Usually three   **B** Yes, it is.   **C** Three years.
      or four metres.

6 A Never.   **B** Yes, it is.   **C** Yes, it does.

5 Match 1–6 with A–F to make sentences.

1 I think it's the giraffe

2 Maybe the monkey

3 I think it's the kangaroo

4 Maybe the cat

5 I think it's the polar bear

6 I think it's the snake

A because it's a pet.

B because it's tall.

C because it lives in a very cold place.

D because it hasn't got legs.

E because it lives in Australia.

F because it climbs trees.

6 Complete the conversation with one word in each gap.

A: Can you help me with this homework? I need to find the odd **1**_____ out.

B: Between these four birds?

A: Yes: a parrot, a penguin, a duck and a chicken.

B: Well, **2**_____ is different?

A: I'm not **3**_____ .

B: Maybe the parrot **4**_____ it lives in the forest. What do you think?

A: I **5**_____ it's the penguin because it doesn't fly.

B: That's true.

A: And it **6**_____ live with people.

B: Yes. Well done!

7 Choose the odd one out and write the reason why.

polar bear   penguin   whale   (cat)

I think it's the cat because it doesn't swim.

1 horse   duck   goat   lion

....

2 cat   mouse   monkey   rabbit

....

3 bat   kangaroo   parrot   duck

....

4 panda   camel   mouse   snake

....

5 lion   elephant   polar bear   hippo

....

3 Animal magic

WRITING

1 Put the words in the correct order to make sentences about frogs.

1 have / make / eggs / don't / they / frogs / nests / but

....

2 jump / can / but / can't / they / walk, / they

....

3 they / in the day / come out / at night / and / hide

....

4 places and / always / don't like / live / cold / they / they / near water

....

5 some / water, / but / they / frogs / under / sleep / can / breathe

....

2 Look at the table. Then read the article and circle the mistakes.

scorpions

Where do they live?	in all parts of the world, but not Antarctica
	in caves, jungles, forests and lots in the desert
How big are they?	usually 6 cm long
What do they eat?	insects (e.g. spiders), some eat small animals
When do they feed?	at night
What do you know about them?	• some live in the desert (under the ground)
	• some eat one insect a year
	• sometimes dangerous to people
	• 4–8 babies, live on mother's back

Scorpions

- Scorpions are amazing animals. They live all over the world, but they live in Antarctica. You can find them in jungles, forests and caves, but lots of scorpions live in the desert, under the ground. They go out in the day to look for food.
- Scorpions are usually about 60 cm long.
- Scorpions often eat insects, like spiders, but they don't eat a lot of food.
- Some scorpions only eat one insect in a day.
- Scorpions are never dangerous to people.
- Mother scorpions usually have four to eight babies. Their nests are usually under the ground. The babies live on their father's back.

3 Correct the mistakes in Ex 2. Write complete sentences.

They live all over the world, but they don't live in Antarctica.

1 ....

2 ....

3 ....

4 ....

5 ....

4 Read about cheetahs. Complete the text. Remember to use *and* or *but* to link sentences.

cheetahs

Where do they live?	Africa and parts of Asia
How fast are they?	can run at about 120 km per hour
What do they eat?	usually small animals, birds, sometimes big animals (e.g. antelope, zebra)
What do you know about them?	• long legs, small head
	• run fast, get tired after 300 m, sometimes don't catch food
	• babies are called cubs
	• babies' eyes open at ten days old
	• stay with mother for about two years

Cheetahs

- Cheetahs ___live in Africa and___ parts of Asia. They've got long **1** .... head.
- They are very fast. They can run at about 120 km per hour, **2** .... always catch their food. This is because they **3** .... 300 metres.
- Cheetahs usually eat small animals, **4** .... big animals, like antelope and zebra.
- The babies are called cubs. Their eyes open when **5** .... ten days old. **6** .... with their mother for about two years.

UNIT CHECK

1 Look at the photos and write the animals.

 A
 B
 C

....

 D
 E
 F

....

2 Match the sentences (1–6) with the photos in Ex 1 (A–F).

1 This beautiful animal usually lives in the forest or jungle. It eats meat. ....
2 This animal is big. It lives near lakes or rivers in Africa. ....
3 This animal lives in very cold places. It walks and swims but it doesn't fly. ....
4 This animal swims and flies. It lives near water. ....
5 This animal is small and brown. It's got a hard shell and it sometimes swims. ....
6 This animal doesn't live in cold places. It lives in a big group and it flies. ....

3 Complete the definitions. Use adverbs of frequency.

1 Elephants .... climb trees.
2 Whales .... live in the sea.
3 Cheetahs don't .... catch the animal they run after.
4 Frogs .... come out at night.
5 Ducks .... live on lakes.

4 Rewrite the sentences. Put the adverbs in brackets in the correct place.

1 Whales are big. (always)

....

2 I walk to school. (often)

....

3 Bears swim. (sometimes)

....

4 Cheetahs don't eat at night. (usually)

....

5 We go to the beach in December. (never)

....

6 My aunt is in her car. (always)

....

5 Read the notes and complete the questions.

......What are they...... called?

> Asiatic Lions

1 .... live?

> India

2 .... eat?

> big animals (e.g. goats, buffaloes) and smaller animals

3 .... look for food?

> usually during the day

4 .... are the cubs when they leave their mothers?

> about two years old

5 .... know about them?

> • male lions are up to 2.9 m long
> • only 500 wild Asiatic lions
> • live in or near forest in Gujarat
> • live for 18–20 years

4 Let's explore

VOCABULARY 1

buildings and places in town

1 Look at the picture and write the places.

A ....
B ....
C ....
D ....
E ....
F ....

2 Complete the table with these words.

museum   ~~park~~   shopping centre   souvenir shop   sports centre   square

activity	places
go for a walk	..........park.........., **1** ....
do sport	**2** ...., swimming pool, park
learn something	school, **3** ....
buy something	**4** ...., supermarket, **5** ....

3 Look at the map. Complete the sentences with *opposite, near* or *next to.*

1 The bank is .... the market.
2 The bus station is .... the bank.
3 Rooky's café is .... the sports centre.
4 The museum is .... the park.
5 The bank is .... the swimming pool.
6 The hospital is .... the sports centre.

4 Look at the map again. Is it similar to your town/city? Write five sentences like the ones in Ex 3 about your town. Use *opposite, near* or *next to.*

....
....
....
....
....

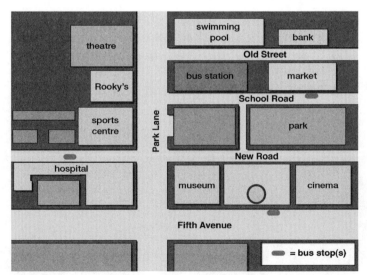

READING

1 Read the article quickly. Match the names (1–4) with the places (A–D).

1	Giolitti's	**A**	square
2	Borghese	**B**	river
3	Navona	**C**	café
4	Tevere	**D**	museum

2 **e** Read the article again. Choose the correct answer for each gap.

1	**A** a	**B** the	**C** one
2	**A** is	**B** am	**C** are
3	**A** don't	**B** often	**C** never
4	**A** Her	**B** My	**C** Me
5	**A** on	**B** at	**C** to

3 Read the article again and answer the questions.

1 What can you eat at Giolitti's café? ....

2 How old is the Pantheon? ....

3 What's outside the Borghese Museum? ....

4 How many bridges are there on the River Tevere? ....

5 What's next to the river? ....

Ask **ANDREW**

What do I do on my first visit to Rome?

This is a question people always ask me. And my answer is, 'Don't worry!' There are lots of amazing things to see and do (and eat!) in Rome. You mustn't try to do them all in one visit. Plan each day of your stay carefully and see the things you like best.

Here are five things you can do in just one day:

- In ¹..... morning, have breakfast at a café. My favourite is Giolitti's. I always go there when I'm in Rome. They serve fantastic ice cream.

- Go and see the Pantheon. It's near Giolitti's, on Rotonda square. The building ²..... almost 2,000 years old!

- Please visit a museum. I know young people ³..... think museums are boring, but the ones in Rome are great. Go to the Borghese Museum. When you finish looking at the paintings, walk around the amazing gardens.

- Have lunch in a square. You must take the time to sit and watch people go by. ⁴..... favourite is Navona Square (Piazza Navona).

- Walk along the River Tevere. There are thirty-one bridges across the river. Take some photos and then go to a restaurant in the evening – there are lots next ⁵..... the river.

And don't forget: throw a coin in the Trevi Fountain. It means you can come back to Rome … and see the things you missed the first time!

GRAMMAR

imperatives

1 Match the sentences with these places.

---

bus stop   cinema   park   playground
river   swimming pool

---

1 Don't feed the ducks. ....

2 Don't play ball games. There are small children. ....

3 Be quiet. Please don't use your mobile. ....

4 Wait here. ....

5 Don't feed the birds. ....

6 Don't run. There's water on the floor. ....

2 Write rules for the places in the photos. Use *please* and the words in brackets.

1 (run) <u>Please don't run in the hospital.</u>

2 (talk in class) ....

3 (eat or drink) ....

4 (take photos) ....

5 (walk on the grass) ....

6 (pick the flowers) ....

must/mustn't

3 Choose the correct words to complete the text.

Welcome to **Happy Health** Sports Centre!

Please read, so everyone can enjoy their visit.

- You **¹must / mustn't** show your member card every time you visit the sports centre.
- Wear the correct clothes and shoes! You **²must / mustn't** have trainers to use the sports centre.
- You **³must / mustn't** leave your bag on the floor. Other visitors can fall over it. Use the cupboards.
- Please don't listen to very loud music. You **⁴must / mustn't** think about other visitors.
- Swimmers **⁵must / mustn't** wear outdoor shoes near the swimming pool.
- You **⁶must / mustn't** use the swimming pool when there are children's classes. Please look at the timetable or ask at reception.

4 Rewrite the sentences. Use *must* or *mustn't*.

Show your ticket at the door.

<u>You must show your ticket at the door.</u>

1 Don't play football here.

....

2 Sit down.

....

3 Don't talk during the film.

....

4 Don't be late.

....

5 Close the doors.

....

5 Complete the rules for your school.

1 Don't be late. You must arrive before .... in the morning.

2 Please wear ....

3 You mustn't have .... in school.

4 At lunchtime you ....

5 When the teacher gives you homework, you ....

6 In the playground, you ....

VOCABULARY 2

vehicles

1 Label the photos with these words.

bus   helicopter   lorry   plane   train   tram

①

....

②

....

③

....

④

....

⑤

....

⑥

....

2 Choose the correct answer, A, B or C.

1 I've got a .... and I always cycle to school.

  A car   **B** bike   **C** lorry

2 I love being in the air. I like ....

  A planes   **B** trams   **C** vans

3 I go by .... to school every day. There's a stop near my house.

  A bike   **B** plane   **C** bus

4 I go by .... to the shopping centre.

  A plane   **B** train   **C** helicopter

5 You can travel fast to different cities on a .... They are fantastic!

  A train   **B** bike   **C** tram

6 My dad takes me to my swimming lessons in his ....

  A plane   **B** car   **C** bike

3 🔊 4.1 Listen and write the type of transport for each person.

1 Erik: ....

2 Erik's dad: ....

3 Erik's mum: ....

4 Erik's sister: ....

5 Erik's uncle: ....

6 Erik's grandparents: ....

4 Complete the article with these words.

bike   by   cars   roads   to   walk

School transport
What can we change?

How do the students at Tanmore High get
¹ .... school? Can we make changes to help
the school and the world around us?

Lots of children go to school ² .... car every
day. It's often difficult to park near the school and it's
dangerous for small children. The ³ .... around
the school are very busy. There are a lot of noisy
⁴ ....

We must ⁵ .... to school more often. It's good
exercise. You can meet your friends in the morning and
chat on your way to school.

The school has a cycle club. You can learn to cycle to
school safely. Don't forget to wear bright clothes and a
helmet when you use your ⁶ ....

5 Tick (✓) the sentences that are true for you. Correct the sentences that are false.

1 I always walk to school.   ☐

....

2 My parents haven't got a car.   ☐

....

3 I don't like cycling.   ☐

....

4 I travel by car every day.   ☐

....

5 I usually travel by train.   ☐

....

LISTENING

1 Look at the picture. Choose these words to complete the sentences.

1 There's a **man** / **woman** with a bike.

2 There are **tables** / **flowers** outside the café.

3 A man is **drinking** / **eating**.

4 There are **four** / **five** people near the train.

2 🔊 4.2 Listen. Where is the train going?

3 ⓔ 🔊 4.3 Listen again. Colour and write.

can/can't; object pronouns

4 Look at the table. Write sentences with *can* or *can't*.

	swim	speak English	play volleyball	run 2 km
Stefan	✗	✓	✓	✗
Mireia	✓	✗	✗	✓
Kirsten	✓	✓	✗	✗

Stefan can't swim. He can speak English. He can play volleyball. He can't run 2 km.

1 Mireia ....
....

2 Kirsten ....
....

5 Match the questions (1–6) with the answers (A–F). Then complete the answers.

1 Can planes fly? ..D..

2 Can a bike go in the air? ....

3 Can you drive a car? ....

4 Can your sister fly a helicopter? ....

5 Can your uncle cycle? ....

6 Can I swim in the sea? ....

A Yes, he ....

B No, it ....

C Yes, you ....

D Yes, they ......can...... .

E No, she ....

F No, I ....

6 Choose the correct words to complete the sentences.

1 That's Sergio. I like **he** / **him** very much.

2 Is this bus stop number sixteen? **I** / **me** want a bus from there.

3 We're near the restaurnt. Can you see **it** / **him**?

4 Marta is happy. **She** / **Her** has got a new bike.

5 My bus is going! Stop! Wait for **I** / **me**!

6 Those flowers are beautiful. Don't walk on **they** / **them**.

SPEAKING

1 🔊 **4.4 Listen and match the places (A–F) with the conversations (1–6).**

2 🔊 **4.5 Listen again and complete the sentences.**

1 He wants <u>to go to the sports centre</u>.
2 She'd like ....
3 He wants ....
4 She wants ....
5 He'd like ....
6 She'd like ....

3 🔊 **4.6 Listen and repeat.**

4 🔊 **4.7 Listen, speak and record. Ask about these places/things.**

> bus stop   park   shopping centre   souvenir shops
> square   taxis   timetables

> Excuse me. Where's the bus stop, please?

5 🔊 **4.8 Listen back and compare.**

6 **Put the words in the correct order to make sentences.**

1 where / please / are / paintings, / the / famous?
....

2 you / please / help / can / me, / you?
....

3 don't / sorry, / I'm / understand / I
....

4 please / you / repeat / that, / can?
....

5 say / that / again, / you / can / please?
....

6 bus / we / to / Trafalgar Square / can / get / a?
....

7 **Complete the conversation with one word in each gap.**

A: Excuse **1**.................... . Can you **2**.................... me?
B: Yes, of course.
A: Where's George Street, **3**.................... ?
B: George Street? You go left at the bank. That's George Street.
A: OK, thanks. I **4**.................... to go to the Science Museum there.
B: Oh! The museum isn't in George Street. It's over there.
A: I'm sorry. I don't **5**.................... .
B: The museum is that big, white building over there. Look, it's next to the children's playground.
A: Oh yes, I can see it! Thanks **6**.................... much.
B: That's OK.

8 🔊 **4.9 Listen and check your answers.**

WRITING

1 Match 1–6 with A–F to make sentences.

1 Where	**A** you get home.
2 Can you come	**B** at the bus station?
3 I'm sorry	**C** to my party?
4 Text me when	**D** are you?
5 See you	**E** I'm late.
6 Can you meet me	**F** in fifteen minutes.

2 Complete the sentences with *to*, *at*, *on* or *in*.

1 Meet us .... the High Street.

2 Can you meet me .... Saturday?

3 See you .... ten o'clock.

4 Is Frank coming .... the cinema?

5 Meet me .... the bus stop.

6 We're at the café .... the square.

3 Complete the email with these words. You do not need two of the words.

are   be   his   me   my   on   to   you

Hi Lisa,

Can you meet ¹........................... and my sister at the café
²........................... Silver Street? It's ³........................... birthday
today! The café is near the bus stop. ⁴........................... there at
three o'clock.

We can have tea and some cake, then go for a walk in the park.
Can you come ⁵........................... the cinema with us later, too?

See ⁶........................... soon.

Olaf

4 Put the message in the correct order (1–5).

.... See you later.

.... Tania

.... Meet me at the swimming pool in Barrack Street.

.... Can you be there at 2.00?

.... Hi Mark,

5 Rewrite the message so it is short and clear.

Dear Karen,

Can you meet your brother Tom after his guitar lesson today?

You need to be at the music room at four o'clock.

See you after I come home from work.

It's very kind of you.

Dad

Hi Karen,

UNIT CHECK

1 Look at the map and complete the crossword.

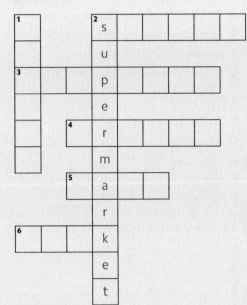
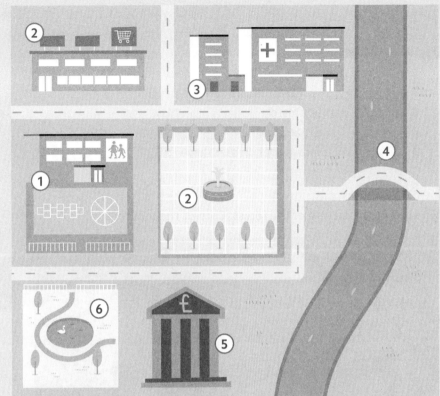

The crossword has the word "supermarket" spelled vertically down position 2, with across answers at positions 1, 3, 4, 5, 6.

2 Complete the diagram with these words.

~~bike~~   boat   helicopter   lorry   plane   van

It's got wheels.

.... bike ....

....

....

It travels in the air.

....

....

It hasn't got wheels.

....

3 Complete the sentences with object pronouns.

1 I'm doing my homework. Don't talk to ....

2 There's a woman. Ask .... to take a photo.

3 Do you want souvenirs? You can buy .... here.

4 David isn't here. Text ....

5 We want to take the bus, too. You can wait with ....

4 Read the answers. Write questions with *can*.

A: <u>Can you play football?</u>

B: Yes, I can. I got two goals last weekend.

1 A: ....

B: Yes, I can. I go to the swimming pool every Saturday.

2 A: ....

B: No, I can't. My sister can. She plays the piano well.

3 A: ....

B: Yes, I can. Do you want to look at my paintings?

4 A: ....

B: No, I can't. But I'd like to learn it and visit Spain.

5 A: ....

B: Yes, I can. I love my bike.

REVIEW: UNITS 1–4

1 Write the missing word.

1 Monday, Tuesday, ... , Thursday, Friday

2 .... , usually, often, sometimes, never

3 January, February, March, ... , May

4 Thursday, Friday, Saturday, ... , Monday

5 get up, have a shower, get dressed, have .... , go to school

6 morning, ... , evening, night

2 Look at the picture of the forest. Correct the sentences.

There's a cave in the jungle.

There's a river in the jungle.

1 There's a monkey in front of a tree.

....

2 There's a frog in the river.

....

3 There are three armadillos in the picture.

....

4 There are some birds flying under the water.

....

5 There's a dolphin in the picture.

....

3 Match the questions (1–6) with the answers (A–F).

1 What's your favourite animal?

2 Have you got any pets?

3 Do you play basketball at school?

4 How often do you walk to school?

5 Where do you have lunch?

6 What time does your school finish?

A Every day.

B At half past three.

C At school.

D No, I haven't.

E Horses.

F Yes, I do.

4 Answer the questions in Ex 3.

1 ....

2 ....

3 ....

4 ....

5 ....

6 ....

5 Complete the conversation with one word in each gap.

A: Is this a photo ¹........................... your cat?

B: Yes, it ²........................... .

A: He's beautiful. What's he called?

B: Pasha. He's ³........................... a Russian name because he's a Russian Blue.

A: How ⁴........................... is he?

B: He's one now. He's still young. He ⁵........................... jumping and playing with toys. And he loves ⁶........................... TV with me!

6 Choose the odd one out.

1 shark   whale   monkey   dolphin
2 river   mountains   sea   lake
3 city   village   bridge   town
4 near   street   opposite   next to
5 sometimes   often   never   today
6 bus stop   bus   taxi   tram

7 Complete the sentences with one word in each gap.

1 When you don't want to use the _____, take the lift.
2 The room you cook in is the _____ .
3 The meal you eat in the morning is _____ .
4 In many countries Saturday and Sunday are the _____ .
5 An animal that lives in water and on land and jumps a lot is a _____ .
6 Cars, vans, motorbikes and lorries travel on the _____ .

8 Choose the correct answer, A, B or C.

1 Where are you from?
  A I'm from Poland.   **B** Polish.   **C** It's Poland.
2 Where do you live?
  A In the museum.   **B** In the playground.   **C** In a village.
3 When do you have guitar lessons?
  A In November.   **B** On Wednesdays.   **C** Yes, I do.
4 What does your cat eat?
  A Fish and meat.   **B** In the garden.   **C** Plants.
5 Where are the toilets, please?
  A They're on the bridge.   **B** They're downstairs.   **C** On the balcony.
6 What time does the train leave?
  A On Tuesday.   **B** Over there.   **C** At eight.

9 Write negative sentences.

Scorpions live in wet places.
Scorpions don't live in wet places.

1 Polar bears eat insects.

_____

2 Elephants are small.

_____

3 There are penguins in the desert.

_____

4 Play volleyball at the children's playground.

_____

5 Cars can travel on water.

_____

10 Complete the text with one word in each gap.

Welcome to the museum. Would you ____like____ a map?

As you can see, there ¹_____ more than forty rooms in the building, so you ²_____ plan your visit carefully.

My favourite room is the China room. That's number thirty-eight on the map. The shelves are full of beautiful Chinese objects and there are lots of paintings on the ³_____ , too.

The café is here, ⁴_____ to the shop on the first floor.

You're lucky because the museum closes at eight o'clock this evening. We ⁵_____ close at five o'clock, but today there is a special evening opening.

Sorry, can you finish your drink, please? You ⁶_____ eat or drink in the museum. And please ⁷_____ take photos with a flash.

Enjoy your visit!

Fun with food

VOCABULARY 1

food and drink

1 Label the picture with these words.

beans	bread	cheese	fruit	milkshake	salad

1 ....
2 ....
3 ....
4 ....
5 ....
6 ....

2 Complete the table with these words.

apples   carrots   lemonade   milk   onions   oranges
pineapples   potatoes   water

fruit	vegetables	drinks

3 Look at the table in Ex 2 again. Think of three more fruits, vegetables and drinks that can go in the table.

4 Choose the correct words to complete the sentences.

1 Enjoy your chicken **salad / juice**.
2 Would you like some chocolate **sauce / cheese**?
3 I've got a **cheese / rice** sandwich for lunch.
4 Do you like **onion / pineapple** soup?
5 I'm having pasta with **chicken / oranges**.
6 I'd like a **banana / tomato** milkshake, please.

All about
Pancake Day

A report for Thornton School by Louise Martin

Today we're celebrating Pancake Day. So what is almost everyone doing after school this afternoon? Why do we do it? Let's ask my mum.

(A) I'm mixing the ingredients for pancakes. I've got eggs, milk and flour in here. I'm mixing them all really well. I'm not cooking the pancakes now. I wait for half an hour first.

(B) We make pancakes because it is the last Tuesday before Lent starts. Lent is a religious festival which happens every year. Traditionally, in Lent people don't eat things like eggs or butter. They make pancakes because they want to finish the food in the house. Today, in Lent people often don't eat the things they really like. So this year I'm not eating chocolate in Lent — that's forty days!

(C) 'It's time to cook the pancakes now. Cooking is the difficult part! When you're cooking pancakes, you do one side and then you turn them over to cook the other side. You move the pan and throw the pancake in the air. It's called tossing the pancake. It doesn't always work! OK. Ready? Three, two, one! ...

Yum! They're ready! I'm eating my pancakes with lemon juice and sugar. What about you?

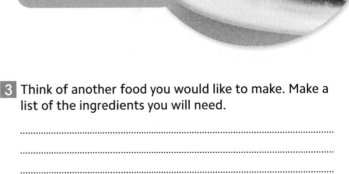

READING

1 Read the report. Match the questions (1–3) with the paragraphs (A–C).

1 Why do people make pancakes? ....

2 What is pancake tossing? ....

3 What are you doing? ....

2 **e** Read the report again. Complete the sentences with one, two or three words in each gap.

A Louise's mum is mixing eggs, ... milk .... and flour.

1 Louise's mum .... for half an hour before she cooks the pancakes.

B 2 Pancake Day is always on ....

3 People make pancakes to .... in the house.

4 Louise's mum .... chocolate in Lent this year.

C 5 Cooking pancakes is .... because you need to turn them over by throwing them in the air.

6 Louise is .... pancakes with lemon juice and sugar.

3 Think of another food you would like to make. Make a list of the ingredients you will need.

....

....

....

....

....

45

GRAMMAR

present continuous

1 Put the sentences about Bob's morning in the correct order (1–6).

A It's half past seven. Bob is having breakfast. ....

B Bob is in the bathroom. He's having a shower. ....

C It's six o'clock. Bob is still sleeping. ....

D Bob is getting dressed. ....

E Bob is closing the door. He's going to work. ....

F Bob is getting up. ....

2 Which sentence from Ex 1 (A-F) does the picture show?

3 Complete the sentences with the present continuous form of the verbs in brackets.

1 I .... (cook) pancakes.

2 We .... (have) dinner at a restaurant.

3 My brother .... (help) me to make breakfast.

4 I .... (wait) for my meal to arrive.

5 My dad .... (make) my favourite sandwiches.

6 The girls .... (sit) next to the river.

4 Write negative sentences.

1 They're shopping for food.

....

2 We're having lunch.

....

3 I'm watching a film.

....

4 My mum is listening to music.

....

5 My granddad is wearing jeans.

....

6 The students are doing an exercise.

....

5 Make questions. Use the words in brackets. Then complete the short answers.

A: ....Are you watching TV........ ? (you / watch TV)

B: No, ...I'm not..... . I'm playing a game.

1 A: .... to Edinburgh? (he / take the train)

B: No, ... He's flying. He's on the plane now.

2 A: .... ? (they / make a cake)

B: No, ... They're cooking dinner.

3 A: .... ? (you / learn the piano)

B: No, ... I'm having singing lessons.

4 A: .... ? (she / draw a picture)

B: No, ... She's writing.

5 A: .... ? (they / play a game)

B: No, ... They're watching TV.

6 Complete the email with the present continuous form of the verbs in brackets.

Hi Mum and Dad,

It's day six at Cooking Camp and I **¹** .... (learn) a lot. Today a chef **²** .... (visit) the camp. He **³** .... (teach) us to make pancakes. It's difficult, but I'm trying hard.

The chef usually works at a big restaurant in London, so we're very happy that he's here today. We **⁴** .... (have) a break at the moment, then it's our turn to cook some pancakes for lunch!

See you next week.

Love,

Sam

P.S. I **⁵** .... (send) a picture with this email. We **⁶** .... (watch) the chef really carefully!

7 Answer the questions about you.

1 What are you learning at the moment?

....

2 Are you wearing jeans today?

....

3 Who is sitting next to you right now?

....

4 What are you thinking about?

....

5 Is it raining?

....

VOCABULARY 2

the weather

1 Label the map with these words.

cloudy   foggy   raining   snowing   sunny   windy

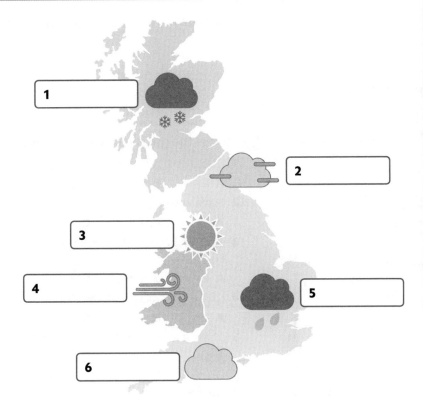

1
2
3
4
5
6

2 What's the weather like? Complete the sentences.

35° In Madrid it's very ....hot........ and ....sunny........ .

10° 1 In London it's .... and it's ....

22° 2 In Ankara it's .... and ....

-8° 3 In Warsaw it's very .... and it's ....

3 Put the letters in the correct order to make seasons.

1 prinsg   ....
2 reumms   ....
3 ntuaum   ....
4 reinwt   ....

4 Look at the table and complete the sentences.

Seasons in Britain

	Spring March April May
	Summer June July August
	Autumn September October November
	Winter December January February

In Britain, July is in the .....summer..... .

1 September is in the ....
2 January is in the ....
3 August is in the ....
4 March is in the ....
5 February is in the ....

5 🔊 5.1 Listen to Thais talking to her British friend. Answer the questions.

1 What's the weather like in London?
....

2 What's the weather like in São Paulo?
....

3 When is autumn in São Paulo?
....

4 When is winter?
....

5 What's the weather like in spring in São Paulo?
....

6 Why does Jessica want to visit Brazil at Christmas time?
....

LISTENING

1 🔊 **5.2 Listen to two people at a music festival. Are the sentences true (T) or false (F)?**

1 The weather is cloudy. ....

2 Nick is Ellen's favourite member of the band. ....

3 Alice sometimes sings. ....

4 Mark plays lots of different instruments. ....

5 May is Lucy's cousin. ....

6 Tom is the boy's brother. ....

2 e 🔊 **5.3 Listen again. Match the names with the people in the picture.**

Lucy   Mark   Nick

Alice   Tom   May

countable and uncountable nouns with *a/some/any*

3 **Complete the table with these words.**

banana   bread   carrot   fruit
meat   potato   rice   sandwich

countable	uncountable

4 **Choose the correct answer, A, B or C.**

1 I need to buy .... bread for my lunch.

A a   **B** some   **C** any

2 Have we got .... lemons?

A an   **B** any   **C** a

3 You can have .... tomatoes with your chicken.

A an   **B** some   **C** any

4 I'd like .... chicken sandwich, please.

A any   **B** some   **C** a

5 There aren't .... grapes in the fruit salad.

A any   **B** an   **C** a

6 Dad has .... egg for his breakfast at the weekend.

A some   **B** an   **C** any

5 **Compete the sentences with *a*, *an*, *some* or *any*.**

1 I usually have .... pasta for lunch.

2 My little brother doesn't want .... sandwich, thanks.

3 We'd like .... apple juice with our meal.

4 Are there .... beans in this soup?

5 Sorry, we haven't got .... lemonade today.

6 Can I have .... apple, please?

SPEAKING

1 🔊 5.4 **Listen to two students talking about a picture. Tick (✓) the questions you hear.**

A Is it raining in picture A? ☐

B How do you say this in English? ☐

C Can you repeat that? ☐

D Are there any flowers in picture B? ☐

E What's the English for this weather? ☐

F Has the woman got a dog in picture A? ☐

2 **Put the words in the correct order to make sentences about a picture.**

1 the / it's / picture / on the right / snowing / in

....

2 is / picture B / man / listening / in / the / to / music

....

3 under / in / a tree / first picture / the / the dog / is

....

4 rucksack / on the left / the / picture / green / in / is / the

....

5 in / boy / sunglasses / is / second picture / the / wearing / the

....

6 five / in / are / sandwiches / picture A / there / plate / on / the

....

3 🔊 5.5 **Listen and answer the questions about picture A.**

1	4 ....
2	5 ....
3	6 ....

4 **Look at picture B and find six differences. Complete the sentences.**

In picture B there isn't <u>a cat on the girl's bag. There's a dog</u> .

1 In picture B the man isn't ....

2 In picture B the woman hasn't ....

3 In picture B the flowers ....

4 In picture B the man ....

5 In picture B the girls ....

WRITING

1 Match 1–6 with A–F to make phrases for an application form.

1	first	**A**	phone number
2	block	**B**	name
3	mobile phone	**C**	name
4	email	**D**	capitals
5	last	**E**	address
6	home	**F**	number

2 Read the letter. Complete the application form for a cookery course.

> 21 Greenway Road
> London
> E12 6VB
>
> Dear Mr Stephens,
>
> My name is Louis Rabier and I'm fourteen. I'd like to apply for the cookery course.
>
> My favourite type of food is French food because my dad is from France. I want to learn to cook new dishes and sauces.
>
> Please send the application form to the address above or my email: louislovescooking@rmt.com. My phone number at home is 0171 564 312.
>
> Thank you,
>
> Louis

Le Parisien
COOKERY SCHOOL

APPLICATION FORM

Please write your name in BLOCK CAPITALS.

First name:	LOUIS
Last name:	¹
Age:	²
Address (with postcode):	21 Greenway Road, London, ³
Home phone number:	⁴
Email address:	⁵
Why do you want to come to the school?	I love French food and want to learn to cook new dishes.

3 Read the advert for a competition. Are the sentences true (T) or false (F)?

Plan a
sandwich party

Do you like eating sandwiches? What about making them? Are you the sandwich expert in your family?

Send us your ideas for an amazing sandwich party and you can win free lunches for a month at our brilliant café, Sandy's Sandwiches.

Fill in the application form and describe your party in thirty words. Remember to surprise us with some different ideas! Write about what sandwiches you want, what time you want to start, how many people you want to invite and where you want to have the party.

You must be twelve years old or older. The last date for applications is 30 November.

1 The competition is about inventing a new sandwich. ....
2 The winner can eat at the café for a month without paying. ....
3 The name of the café is Sunday's Sandwiches. ....
4 You must write twenty words about your party. ....
5 You can't enter the competition if you are eleven. ....

4 Read the advert in Ex 3 again. What must you write about in your description? Tick the correct options.

1 who you want to come to the party ☐
2 how old you are ☐
3 how many people you want ☐
4 the time the party starts ☐
5 where the party is ☐
6 the food you want ☐

5 Write your party description for the competition in Ex 3.

UNIT CHECK

1 Write these drinks in the correct group.

hot chocolate   lemonade   orange juice   soup   tea   water

1 hot weather: .... , ... , ...
2 cold weather: .... , ... , ...

2 What is the best food for each person? Read the sentences and match these foods with the people.

bean and meat soup   cheese sandwich   chicken salad
chicken sandwich   meat with vegetables and potatoes

1 Todd isn't very hungry. He likes cheese. ....
2 Evan would like a sandwich. He can't eat food made from milk.

....
3 Francesca would like some hot food. She doesn't like potatoes or pasta. ....
4 Rob is hungry. He eats meat and doesn't like salad, cheese or beans. ....
5 Val would like a cold meal. She doesn't eat bread.

....

3 Look at the table. Complete the sentences with one word in each gap.

	Buenos Aires, Argentina	London, England
spring	September–November 22°	March–May 13°
summer	December–February 29°	June–August 20°
autumn	March–May 23°	September–November 10°
winter	June–August 16°	December–February 7°

In Buenos Aires in the ...summer... it's hot and sunny.
1 In London in the .... it's usually cool and windy.
2 It often rains in London in the ....
3 In July in Buenos Aires it's sometimes .... and it's cool.
4 .... in Argentina is from June to August.
5 In January in London it's snowy and ....

4 Complete the sentences with the present continuous form of these verbs.

fly   have   make   shop   sit   wear

1 It's spring in Scotland. It's windy, so we .... kites today.
2 It's winter in Brazil. I .... on the beach, drinking juice.
3 It's the Day of the Dead in Mexico. My mum .... sugar skulls.
4 It's winter in England. My friends and I .... hot chocolate to drink.
5 It's summer in Australia. I .... for some new sunglasses!
6 It's autumn in the USA. We .... fancy dress for Trick or Treat.

5 Read the conversation. Choose the correct answer for each gap.

A: Have we got everything for the barbecue?
B: Let's see. There are **1**...... burgers and sausages.
A: What about bread? Is there **2**...... bread?
B: Yes, we've got some white bread and brown bread, too.
A: Great. **3**...... there any cheese?
B: No. There isn't **4**...... . I can text my dad.
A: What type of fruit **5**...... there?
B: There **6**...... some apples and pineapples.
A: Brilliant! I think we're almost ready.

1	**A** any	**B** some	**C** a
2	**A** any	**B** some	**C** a
3	**A** Are	**B** Is	**C** Have
4	**A** some	**B** no	**C** any
5	**A** are	**B** have	**C** is
6	**A** are	**B** have	**C** is

6 Write sentences about your fridge. Use *There's / There are* or *There isn't / There aren't*.

There are some oranges.

VOCABULARY 1

adjectives to describe things

1 Write sentences about the photos. Use two of these adjectives in each sentence.

beautiful   clean   dirty   loud   new   old   ugly   young

1 ....
2 ....
3 ....
4 ....

2 Choose the correct words to complete the sentences.

1 I'm very thirsty. I'd like a **large / loud** milkshake, please.

2 We love the new museum in town. It's really **interesting / boring**.

3 Your brother is **loud / quiet**, isn't he? He never says a word.

4 Our dog is old now. She's very **quick / slow** when she walks.

5 Don't watch that DVD. It's **boring / interesting**.

6 I can't do this maths homework. It's very **easy / difficult**.

3 Read and text and write the gadgets next to the names.

'Hi! My name's Alfie. There are always lots of gadgets in our kitchen. What is there today? Well, there's my mobile phone on the table. It's a bit dirty. That large, heavy laptop is Kate's. It's pretty old ... My mum always brings her tablet to the kitchen. It's very loud!

The radio is my dad's. He loves old things. Those are my grandad's records, next to the radio. He has the coolest things!

1 Alfie: ....   4 Kate: ....

2 Dad: ....   5 Mum: ....

3 Grandad: ....

READING

1 Jenny is visiting the School Museum. Read the first paragraph of the article and answer the questions.

1 When was the school trip?

....

2 What year is the class learning about?

....

3 Where is the museum?

....

3 Choose the best title for the article in Ex 2.

1 My favourite school trip

2 Family life in the past

3 A very different school

2 **e** Read the article. Choose a word below. Write the correct words next to numbers 1–5.

Last week we were at the School Museum. What an interesting place! You can travel back in time there and be a school child in 1837. The school is in a ......_village_...... and it's very different from our school.

The school is in an old **1**........................... . Inside there's one very large classroom called the School Room. In 1837 there were 200 children in this room, and there was only one teacher in the class. The desks were really **2**........................... and old-fashioned, and they were all facing the front.

At the School Museum there is a real teacher, so you can have a lesson in the school room. You sit at the desks and try writing with the **3**........................... with real ink. The lesson we were in at the School Museum was **4**........................... and boring. And all my answers were wrong!

Life for school children in the past wasn't fun. After school the children were busy working for their families. There wasn't much free time and, of course, there weren't any gadgets like TVs or **5**........................... .

pens

laptops

$$2+2 = \left\{\left\{x \to \frac{1}{5}\right.\right.$$
$$\left.\left.(-1-\sqrt{31})\right\}\right\}$$

easy

difficult

building

small

new

quiet

village

GRAMMAR

past simple: *be*

1 Complete the sentences with *is, are, was* or *were*.

1 In 1837 there .... musical instruments, but no TVs.

2 There .... usually about thirty children in modern British classes.

3 .... there any whiteboards at school in the 1830s?

4 There .... a lot of work to do. Let's start!

5 Why .... she away from school yesterday?

2 Rewrite the sentences in the past simple.

There isn't a supermarket in the village.

<u>There wasn't a supermarket in the village.</u> ....

1 There aren't any TVs at the school.

....

2 The lesson isn't very interesting.

....

3 Old computers aren't very quick.

....

4 The weather isn't nice.

....

5 My parents aren't happy with me.

....

3 Complete the blog with the correct form of *was* or *were*.

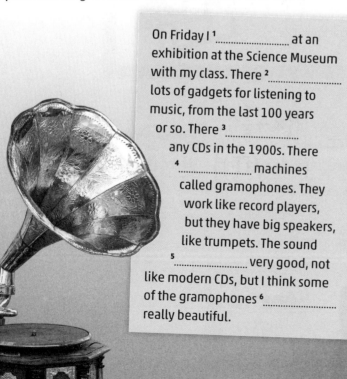

On Friday I ¹.......................... at an exhibition at the Science Museum with my class. There ².......................... lots of gadgets for listening to music, from the last 100 years or so. There ³.......................... any CDs in the 1900s. There ⁴.......................... machines called gramophones. They work like record players, but they have big speakers, like trumpets. The sound ⁵.......................... very good, not like modern CDs, but I think some of the gramophones ⁶.......................... really beautiful.

4 Alice and Beth are looking at an old photo of their city. Complete the conversation with *was, wasn't, were* or *weren't*.

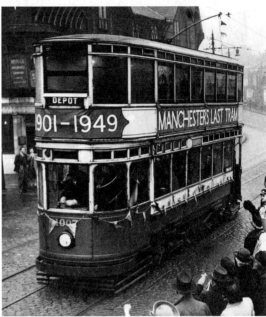

DEPOT

901-1949 ➤ MANCHESTERS LAST TRAM

A: Wow! The city ¹.......................... very different in the 1940s.

B: Yes. What ².......................... those things? They look like buses.

A: They ³.......................... called trams, I think.

B: There ⁴.......................... any cars in the city centre.

A: You're right. There ⁵.......................... .

B: And all the people are wearing hats in this photo. Look!

A: Yes, hats ⁶.......................... very popular.

5 Write short answers about you and your family.

1 Were your parents born in the 1990s?

....

2 Was your grandad in a pop group when he was young?

....

3 Was there just one teacher at your school yesterday?

....

4 Were you a beautiful baby?

....

5 Were there any good programmes on TV last night?

....

6 Was your last English homework difficult?

....

VOCABULARY 2

things we do (verbs)

1 Read the clues and complete the crossword.

		¹c		
		h		
²	³	a		
		n		
		g		
⁴	⁵	e		
⁶				
⁷				

Across

3 We s................ in our cousins' house on holiday.

4 You can t................ from London to Paris by boat or plane.

7 When does the bus a................ in the town centre?

Down

1 After I play football, I change... my clothes.

2 Do you often t................ your friends on your new mobile?

5 Does Jo usually v................ her grandmother on Sunday?

6 I live near my school, so I w................ there every morning.

2 Match 1–6 with A–F to make sentences.

1 Ethan travels to his grandfather's house   **A** by car.

2 He usually arrives   **B** the garage together.

3 They talk about   **C** in the morning.

4 They sometimes tidy   **D** football.

5 Ethan helps his grandad   **E** the dog!

6 Then they wash   **F** in the garden.

3 Read the text. Choose the correct answer for each gap.

> I always ¹...... my cousins in the spring. They live near the beach. I ²...... for a week. I ³...... there by car with my mum and dad. It's a long trip and we usually ⁴...... in the evening. I ⁵...... on the beach every day with my cousins and we ⁶...... for hours.

1 **A** talk   **B** visit   **C** arrive

2 **A** arrive   **B** am   **C** stay

3 **A** ride   **B** walk   **C** travel

4 **A** arrive   **B** stay   **C** help

5 **A** wash   **B** walk   **C** visit

6 **A** talk   **B** wash   **C** change

4 🔊 6.1 Listen and complete the sentences about Cristina's favourite day. Use three words in each gap, including these verbs.

arrive   clean   help   stay   visit   wash

1 On Saturdays Cristina gets up and she ....

2 .... dad at the market in the town centre.

3 They .... o'clock to set up their stall.

4 Cristina .... market all morning.

5 Her friends ....

6 After the market Cristina and her dad ....

LISTENING

1 Read the information and answer the questions.

The **Jorvik Viking Centre** is in York, England. The museum tells the story of the city when the Vikings lived there. The name 'Viking' is from the area called Viki in Oslo Fjord, in modern Norway. The museum is famous for its 'time travel' train rides, which help visitors to experience life in Viking times.

1 Where is the museum? ....

2 Where were the Vikings from? ....

3 Why is the museum famous? ....

2 e ◀)) 6.2 Listen and choose the correct answer, A, B or C.

1 Where was the museum?

 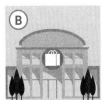

2 Who was on the Time Machine train?

3 What was there inside the Time Machine train?

4 What was typical Viking food?

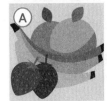 

5 What was in the garden of the house?

past simple: regular verbs

3 Complete the table with past simple form of these verbs.

~~arrive~~   carry   change   stay   stop   talk   tidy   travel

+ -*ed*	
double consonant + -*ed*	
change -*y* to -*ied*	
+ -*d*	arrived,

4 Write negative sentences.

1 John Lennon played the drums.

....

2 Columbus arrived in America in 1942.

....

3 Julius Caesar travelled by bus.

....

4 In 1750 people cleaned their teeth every day.

....

5 Children played computer games in 1960.

....

5 Complete the article with the past simple form of these verbs.

arrive   change   help   not talk   not travel   wash

A pop star but not to his mum and dad!

Mason is a famous pop star, but he lives with his parents. He [1]........................... home from a concert yesterday evening. He doesn't like flying, so yesterday he [2]........................... by helicopter, like most pop stars. His parents picked him up at the train station.

At home, Mason [3]........................... his clothes and he [4]........................... his hair. Then he relaxed with his parents. He [5]........................... much because he was tired from singing.

Mason likes cooking, so later he [6]........................... his parents to make dinner. 'At home he is just Mason, not a pop star,' say his mum and dad.

SPEAKING

1 Two friends are talking about their weekend. Complete the conversation with *last*, *on*, *in* or nothing (–).

A: Hi! How was your weekend?

B: It was good, thanks. I was at my cousin's house **1**........................... Saturday.

A: Didn't you go there **2**........................... weekend?

B: Yes, we visit them every weekend. What about you?

A: I was at a concert **3**........................... night. I played the piano.

B: Wow! I didn't know you play the piano.

A: I started playing **4**........................... year. What did you do **5**........................... yesterday?

B: I stayed at home and finished my history project.

A: The one about Europe **6**........................... the 1960s? That's great! I'm still working on it.

2 Match 1–6 with A–F to make questions.

1	What about	**A**	or false?
2	Is that	**B**	right answer?
3	What do you	**C**	you?
4	What's the	**D**	right?
5	Is that true	**E**	know the answer?
6	Do you	**F**	think?

3 Read the questions. Choose the correct answer, A, B or C.

1 Is the answer true or false?

  A It isn't.   **B** Yes.   **C** It's true.

2 Have you got the answer?

  A I'm not sure.   **B** Very well.   **C** Very good.

3 I think the answer is 0555.

  A I didn't.   **B** That's right.   **C** Not really.

4 What do you think?

  A Yes, I do.   **B** I don't know.   **C** I'm sure.

5 Is 'in the 1920s' the right answer?

  A I don't think so.   **B** That's stupid.   **C** Very bad.

6 I got all the questions right.

  A Very well.   **B** Very right.   **C** Very good.

4 🔊 6.3 Listen to two students talking about a quiz. Tick (✓) the phrases you hear.

1 What about you?	☐	**5** Well done!	☐
2 I think I do.	☐	**6** Yes, that's right.	☐
3 I'm not sure.	☐	**7** That's false.	☐
4 I think the answer is …	☐	**8** That's a good idea.	☐

5 Complete the conversation with the phrases in Ex 4.

A: I'm having problems with the history homework. You know, the quiz about the Romans. Do you know the answers?

B: Yes, **1**................................. . I watched a programme about the Romans last week. Let's do the quiz together.

A: **2**................................. The first question is, 'Where were the first Romans from?'

B: **3**................................. Italy.

A: Italy? **4**................................. I remember now. The second question is, 'What language did the Romans speak?'

B: **5**................................. What do you think?

A: Is it Latin?

B: Yes, it is. You've got two questions right already. **6**.................................

6 🔊 6.4 Listen again and check your answers.

WRITING

1 Complete the questions you can ask about a past visit or trip.

1 .... was it?
2 .... were you with?
3 .... did you travel there?
4 .... did you arrive?
5 .... you see and do?
6 .... your opinion of the trip?

2 Match the notes (A–F) with the questions in Ex 1 (1–6).

A   very interesting place; the countryside was beautiful ....

B   travelled to the island on a boat ....

C   arrived at ten o'clock in the morning ....

D   listened to information about the history of the lighthouse, climbed to the top (119 stairs) ....

E   Red Point Lighthouse on an island near Scotland ..1..

F   with my parents ....

3 Complete Katia's blog post with one word in each space. Use the notes in Ex 2.

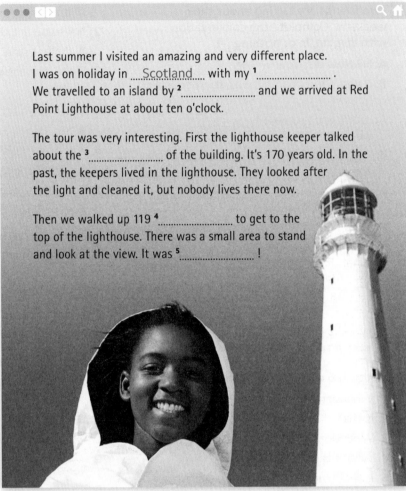

Last summer I visited an amazing and very different place. I was on holiday in ___Scotland___ with my ¹........................... . We travelled to an island by ²........................... and we arrived at Red Point Lighthouse at about ten o'clock.

The tour was very interesting. First the lighthouse keeper talked about the ³........................... of the building. It's 170 years old. In the past, the keepers lived in the lighthouse. They looked after the light and cleaned it, but nobody lives there now.

Then we walked up 119 ⁴........................... to get to the top of the lighthouse. There was a small area to stand and look at the view. It was ⁵...........................!

4 Write notes about an imaginary visit. Use the questions and the ideas to help you. Then write a blog post about your visit. Add your own ideas.

1 When were you there?

• last month   • last week   • last weekend   • last year

2 What was the place?

• a cave   • a city   • a mountain   • an adventure park   • a palace

3 How did you travel there?

• boat   • bus   • car   • helicopter   • plane   • train

4 When did you arrive?

• at midnight   • in the afternoon   • in the evening   • in the morning

5 What did you see and do? Choose adjectives to describe the trip.

• beautiful   • exciting   • fun   • interesting   • modern

Last month I visited …

UNIT CHECK

1 Choose the correct words to complete the sentences.

1 My dad was really **surprised** / **fun** by the present.
2 I love listening to music on my grandparents' old **record** / **radio** player.
3 Our trip to the mountains was really **modern** / **exciting**.
4 You should visit that museum. It's **terrible** / **fun**.
5 The park is boring. Can we go to a **modern** / **different** place?
6 You need a **new** / **easy** mobile phone. Yours is old-fashioned.

2 Complete the hotel review with the opposites of the words in brackets.

★☆☆☆☆ Reviewed yesterday

Excelsior hotel

This hotel is ....difficult.... (easy) to find. It's in a dark, [1] .... (clean) street near the bus station.

Our room was very [2] .... (large) and we didn't sleep all night because the buses were really [3] .... (quiet) outside the window. The room service was very [4] .... (quick), too.

Our stay at this hotel was [5] .... (excellent), so we give it one star.

3 Complete the table with these verbs.

~~arrive~~   clean   help   text   tidy   travel   stay   visit   walk

....arrive....	at my aunt and uncle's house
[1]	
[2]	my bedroom
[3]	
[4]	
[5]	my friends
[6]	
[7]	to my grandparents' house
[8]	

4 Complete the sentences with *was*, *wasn't*, *were* or *weren't*.

1 The bus .... clean and modern.
2 There .... twenty-five people at the party yesterday.
3 .... that your brother on TV last night?
4 My teacher .... happy because I talked in class.
5 .... the questions difficult?
6 There .... any CD players until 1982.

5 Match the questions (1–6) with the answers (A–F).

1 Were the cats happy to see you? ....
2 Was the town busy on Saturday morning? ....
3 Was your sister at the cinema? ....
4 Were you and your brother in bed at ten o'clock? ....
5 Was Daniel in class yesterday? ....
6 Were the questions difficult? ....

A Yes, we were.
B Yes, they were.
C Yes, he was.
D No, they weren't.
E Yes, she was.
F Yes, it was.

6 Look at the table and complete the sentences about last weekend.

	visit grandparents	tidy room	play volleyball
David	✓	✗	✗
Nerea	✗	✓	✓
Alba	✓	✗	✓

1 David .... his grandparents.
2 Nerea .... her grandparents.
3 Nerea and Alba .... volleyball.
4 David .... volleyball.
5 David and Alba .... their rooms.
6 Nerea .... her room.

REVIEW: UNITS 1–6

1 Write these words in the correct group.

bee cake car carrot lorry milk sheep van whale

vehicles	animals	food and drink

2 Complete the sentences with the missing verbs.

1 Sorry, I don't .... Could you repeat that?

2 Do you usually .... football at school?

3 At the weekend I always .... my friends at the shopping centre.

4 I'd like to .... a party on my birthday.

5 Can you .... me, please? I want to go to the bank, but I don't know where it is.

6 How do you .... 'viajar' in English?

3 Choose the correct words to complete the sentences.

1 Be quiet! I **'m doing / do** my homework.

2 You **must / mustn't** play your drums at night.

3 Are there **any / an** onions in the cupboard?

4 What **are / is** he watching on TV?

5 I **enjoy / 'm enjoying** this book.

6 My grandmother can **speak / speaking** English.

4 Match the questions (1–6) with the answers (A–F).

1 What's your last name?
2 Where are my trainers?
3 What's the date today?
4 Where do lions live?
5 When do you have science?
6 What's your favourite city?

A On Wednesday afternoon.
B In Africa and India.
C In the living room.
D Rome.
E Reynolds.
F 23 July.

5 Read the answers. Write the questions.

A: What's your address?
B: 34 Oak Street, Peterborough.

1 A: ....
B: I'm fine, thanks.

2 A: ....
B: Pandas eat bamboo.

3 A: ....
B: The supermarket? It's on Edward Street.

4 A: ....
B: It's raining.

5 A: ....
B: My sister? She's doing her homework.

6 Complete the conversation with one word in each gap.

A: Hi! Are you .....enjoying..... the festival?

B: Yes, it's great. [1]........................... you usually come here.

A: Yes, I come every winter.

B: [2]........................... is my cousin, Kasia.

C: Hi! Do you go to the same school as Ala?

A: Yes, I [3]........................... .

C: Pardon?

A: Sorry! I'm [4]........................... cake. Yes, we go to the same school.

C: Ha ha! OK.

A: [5]........................... you staying with Ala at the moment?

C: Yes, I am.

7 Choose the odd one out.

1 car	bicycle	lorry	van
2 bus stop	museum	exhibition	castle
3 milkshake	lemonade	water	pasta
4 easy	ugly	change	large
5 forest	river	lake	sea
6 interesting	fun	boring	exciting

8 Label the photos with the correct words.

clock

....

....

....

....

....

9 Match the sentences (1–6) with the photos in Ex 8 (A–F).

1 It usually sleeps during the day and it lives in caves. ....

2 It's something you use in the morning to wash. ....

3 It's a place where it doesn't often rain. ....

4 It helps you to tell the time. ....

5 It travels on the road. ....

6 It helps you to walk across a river. ....

10 Choose the correct answer, A, B or C.

1 The train .... arrive at 9.30.

   A wasn't   **B** isn't   **C** didn't

2 She .... her parents after the party.

   A text   **B** texted   **C** did text

3 They .... us to cook dinner.

   A didn't help   **B** helps   **C** not helped

4 We .... a film last night, but it wasn't very good.

   A watched   **B** was watching   **C** watch

5 Michele .... play computer games before bed.

   A must   **B** mustn't   **C** isn't

6 We .... go to school on Sundays.

   A doesn't   **B** aren't   **C** don't

11 Complete the text with one word in each gap.

Happy birthday, Grandma!

.......On....... Saturday it was my grandmother's birthday, so I ¹........................ her with my family. Her house is really old and beautiful, with ²........................ of the family on the walls.

My grandmother has ³........................ three children and seven grandchildren, so we are a big family. We love talking and when we meet we ⁴........................ always very loud!

On Saturday I ⁵........................ my mum to make a birthday cake. It ⁶........................ a lemon cake with chocolate sauce. Grandma really enjoyed our visit and the cake. She ⁷........................ stop smiling all day!

VOCABULARY 1

jobs

1 Look at the picture and complete the sentences with these jobs.

---

artist   basketball player   doctor   farmer
photographer   scientist

A That's my mum. She's a ....

B That's my aunt Lisa. She's a ....

C My uncle Rob is a .... He's got his camera.

D My cousin Bradley wants to be a .... He's very tall!

E That's my grandad. He's a ....

F His wife, my grandma, is an ....

2 Match 1–6 with A–F to make sentences.

1 A singer ....
2 A dentist ....
3 A taxi driver ....
4 A writer ....
5 A nurse ....
6 An app designer ....

A works in a car.
B is good with computers.
C is good at music.
D works in a hospital.
E looks at people's teeth.
F is good with words.

3 Think of six jobs. Do you want to do these jobs? Why/Why not? Write sentences.

Musician – I don't want to be a musician because I can't play an instrument.

....

....

....

....

....

....

READING

1 Read the article quickly. Find these things.

1 the name of the boy who had a 'big idea':
....

2 the name of the invention: ....

3 the names of two books: ...., ...

2 ⓔ Read the article again. Complete the sentences with one, two, three or four words in each gap.

1 Chris is from the ....

2 Chris made a special basketball to .... children to play well.

3 There was a .... Chris's school for young inventors.

4 A .... Chris's idea.

5 Chris was in a book called *Kids Inventing* and he became ....

6 Chris .... called *Shooting for Your Dreams*.

3 Do you think Chris's idea was a good one? Why/Why not? Write three reasons to support your opinion.

I don't think it was a good idea because ...

....

....

....

4 Can you think of an app or invention that changed your life? Why was it important?

....

....

SMALL BOY, **BIG IDEA**

Chris Haas is from California in the USA. He was born in 1994. Chris's father was a basketball teacher, so Chris learned to play when he was very young.

When he was just nine years old, Chris had an idea which changed his life. He saw children who had problems playing basketball and he wanted to make a special basketball to help them. He painted big hands on a ball and called it the 'hands-on basketball'.

Chris entered the ball in a competition for inventions at his school. He didn't win the prize, but that didn't stop him. His dad helped him to take his special ball to a big sports company. They bought the idea and they made the basketball. Now you can buy the 'hands on basketball' all over the world. Chris became famous because he was in a book called *Kids Inventing*. The book was about young people who make things.

Chris used the money from his invention to pay for himself and his brother and sister to study at university. He also started to help other young people with their projects.

Chris had another idea for a 'hands-on football' to help children learn to play American football. He also wrote a book about his experiences: *Shooting for Your Dreams*. The book tells the amazing story of how a small idea can help thousands of children every day.

GRAMMAR

past simple: irregular verbs

1 Complete the article with the past simple form of the verbs in brackets.

I didn't know that!
Six facts for *Twilight* fans

Stephanie Meyer is a world-famous writer now, but did you know these things about her?

▶ She ¹......................... (have) no experience of writing before *Twilight*.

▶ She ²......................... (write) the first book in just three months.

▶ The idea for *Twilight* ³......................... (come) to her in a dream.

▶ Her sister ⁴......................... (read) the story first and told her to publish it.

▶ Her *Twilight* books ⁵......................... (be) in the Top Ten Bestsellers list for 143 weeks.

2 Rewrite the sentences in the past simple.

2002: the euro goes into circulation.
The euro went into circulation in 2002.

1 2008: Suzanne Collins writes *The Hunger Games*.
....

2 2009: Barack Obama becomes president of the USA.
....

3 2011: Ed Sheeran has his first hit song in England.
....

4 2011: One Direction make their first album.
....

5 2014: Germany win the football World Cup.
....

3 Read the answers. Complete the questions.

1 A: .... you .... Emma?
B: Yes, I did. I saw her at the swimming pool.

2 A: .... you .... the tickets?
B: No, we didn't, sorry. Can you buy them tomorrow?

3 A: .... they .... to the station after lunch?
B: Yes, they did. They went there at half past two.

4 A: .... she .... dinner at home?
B: Yes, she did. She had dinner with her family.

5 A: .... you .... a lot?
B: Yes, I did. I wrote ten pages.

6 A: .... you .... any sandwiches?
B: Yes, we did. We made some cheese sandwiches.

7 A: .... you .... the story?
B: Yes, I did. I read it last night.

4 Write questions in the past simple. Use these verbs.

| live   play   ~~present~~   sing   walk   want |

Sofia Vergara / a travel programme?
Did Sofia Vergara present a travel programme?

1 Justin Timberlake / a song at his wedding?
....

2 Borge Ousland / across the Antarctic?
....

3 Emma Watson / hockey at college?
....

4 Rafael Nadal / to be a tennis player?
....

5 Enrique Iglesias / in Spain when he was young?
....

5 Write short answers about you and your family.

1 Did you write any messages at the weekend?
....

2 Did your parents meet at school?
....

3 Did your teacher give you homework this week?
....

4 Did you buy anything last weekend? What?
....

5 Did your grandparents talk to you yesterday?
....

6 Did you drink juice at breakfast this morning?
....

VOCABULARY 2

irregular verbs

1 Complete the table.

infinitive	past simple
1	gave
2	went
3	learnt
4	saw
5	made
6	took

2 Complete the crossword with the past simple form of the verbs.

1 leave	**5** find
2 think	**6** have
3 say	**7** build
4 can	

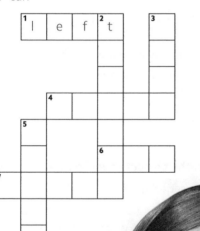

3 Choose the correct answer, A, B or C.

1 Laura .... me a picture for my birthday.

   A had   **B** saw   **C** gave

2 We .... the film was very exciting.

   A thought   **B** could   **C** were

3 I .... some great photos at the concert.

   A wrote   **B** took   **C** made

4 The train for London .... at 10.30.

   A left   **B** bought   **C** learned

5 We .... the football match 5–1.

   A gave   **B** made   **C** won

6 My cousins .... to London last July.

   A said   **B** went   **C** wanted

4 Complete the article with the past simple form of these verbs.

be   can   learn   make   see   write

Alma Deutscher **1**........................ born in 2005. From a very young age she was good at music. Her parents say that she **2**........................ sing before she talked. She **3**........................ to play piano from the age of two and then the violin. Alma started to write her first opera when she was four years old. It was about a pirate called Don Alonzo. In 2011, she **4**........................ a piano sonata.

A famous friend of the family tweeted about Alma in 2012 and Alma quickly became famous herself. Alma **5**........................ an orchestra play her first symphony in 2015 and the BBC **6**........................ a TV programme about her in 2017.

Alma is still a normal girl who loves to play and make up stories.

LISTENING

1 **Look at the photo. Why do you think people built this tower?**

1 to make a new tourist attraction

2 to break a record

3 to get to the top of a building

This tower has 550,000 plastic bricks!

2 e 🔊 7.1 **Listen to two friends talking about the tower. Complete the notes.**

Where the tower was: [1] ...., Italy

How tall it was: [2] .... metres

Number of days to build the tower: [3] ....

Name of the TV presenter who finished the tower:

Alessandro [4] ....

How many euros per centimetre of tower for charity:

[5] ....

What Bruno and his family learnt: to [6] ....

together

past simple: question words

3 **Complete the questions with a question word or *did*.**

1 .... did Bruno go to Milan with?

  A his family

  B his friends

  C his school

2 .... did the bricks come from?

  A England.

  B Denmark.

  C Canada.

3 .... did they start building the tower?

  A 7 June

  B 21 June

  C 17 June

4 .... they leave the bricks in Italy?

  A No, they didn't. They took them to Denmark.

  B No, they didn't. They gave them to children all over the world.

  C Yes, they did.

5 .... did Bruno think when he saw the tower?

  A He thought that children are important.

  B He thought that playing is important.

  C He thought that small things we do are important.

4 🔊 7.2 **Listen again and choose the correct answer in Ex 3, A, B or C.**

5 **Put the words in the correct order to make questions.**

1 that / she / message / did / write / why?

....

2 favourite / was / picture / what / your?

....

3 the / train / did / leave / when?

....

4 did / sister / your / to / go / school / where?

....

5 did / who / see / you / the / café / at?

....

6 you / how / stay / did / long / in / Madrid?

....

7 visit / the museum / did / when / you?

....

8 do / you / what / did / the / in / evening?

....

SPEAKING

1 Look at the pictures of Rita's holiday. Match the questions (1–6) with the answers (A–F).

1 Where did Rita go? ....
2 When did she go there? ....
3 How did she get there? ....
4 Who did she go with? ....
5 What did she do on the first day? ....
6 What did she do the next day? ....

A She went in August.
B She played tennis.
C She went with her parents.
D She went on some rides.
E She went to Paris.
F She travelled by train.

2 Complete the story about Rita's visit to Paris. Use *and*, *but*, *then* or *when*.

Rita went to Paris in August with her parents ¹............................ they had a lot of fun. It was very early on Saturday morning ²............................ they got the train from London. They had breakfast on the train. The first thing they did ³............................ they arrived was go to a famous theme park. It was exciting, ⁴............................ Rita didn't like the rides very much. The next day they played tennis, ⁵............................ they went to visit the Eiffel tower. Rita thought it was beautiful ⁶............................ she took lots of photos at the top.

3 🔊 7.3 Listen to a student telling a story about the pictures. Tick (✓) the questions she answers.

1 What time did they leave? ☐
2 Where did Ben go? ☐
3 Who did he go with? ☐
4 How long did they wait? ☐
5 Who did they see at the airport? ☐
6 What did Ben say? ☐

4 Complete the sentences about the pictures in Ex 3 with these words.

but   knew   last   said   when

1 .... July Ben went on holiday with his family.
2 .... they arrived at the airport, they had to wait a long time for their plane.
3 Then Ben saw a face that he ....
4 'Look! That's Alex Bravo, the Spanish tennis player,' he ....
5 Ben found Alex Bravo's sunglasses, ... Alex didn't want them back.

WRITING

1 Choose the correct words to complete the article.

Daniel Radcliffe

Daniel Jacob Radcliffe **¹is / was** born in 1989 and grew **²on / up** in London. His parents were both actors when they were children.

Daniel didn't **³go / went** to drama school, but he started acting on television when he was ten. He **⁴were / was** in the first Harry Potter film when he was eleven.

⁵But / When he was older, Daniel acted in the theatre in London. Then he went to the USA. He acted and **⁶sang / singed** in a show in a theatre in New York. The show was popular and people started to see him as a talented theatre actor and singer.

2 Read the article in Ex 1 again. Match the questions (1–8) with the answers (A–H).

1 When was Daniel born? ....
2 Where did he grow up? ....
3 When were his parents actors? ....
4 Did Daniel go to drama school? ....
5 When did he start acting on TV? ....
6 How old was he in the first Harry Potter film? ....
7 Did he make films in the USA? ....
8 Did people like his show in New York? ....

A When he was ten years old.
B Yes, they did.
C No, he didn't. He worked in a theatre.
D In 1989.
E When they were young.
F No, he didn't. He went to a regular school.
G He was eleven.
H In London.

3 Read the article and complete the table. Write complete sentences.

Garbiñe Muguruza 🎾

Garbiñe Muguruza is a famous tennis player. Her mother is from Venezuela and her father is Spanish, so she has both Venezuelan and Spanish nationality. Muguruza was born in Venezuela in 1993. She started playing tennis when she was three years old. Three years later, she moved to Spain with her family and studied tennis in Barcelona.

She won the French Open in 2016 and Wimbledon in 2017. After her victory at Wimbledon she said, 'I think people love and hate tennis at the same time. I also feel like that. When you win, everything is beautiful. But when you lose, it's hard.'

What's her name?	Her name is Garbiñe Muguruza.
Where is her father from?	¹ ....
When was she born?	² ....
When did she start to play tennis?	³ ....
What did she win in 2016?	⁴ ....
Why does she love and hate tennis?	⁵ ....

4 Write a biography about Garbiñe Muguruza. Use your answers Ex 3 to help you.

UNIT CHECK

1 Write the infinitive and past simple form of the verbs for each picture.

buy – bought

....

....

....

....

....

2 Complete the sentences with the past simple form of the verbs in brackets.

1 'This competition is fun!' she .... (say).

2 We .... (learn) about famous scientists last week.

3 I .... (can) hear my little brother from the next room.

4 They .... (build) a robot that could talk.

5 He .... (do) the exercises, but the answers were wrong.

6 I .... (go) on holiday with my grandparents in August.

3 Complete the article with the past simple form of these verbs.

know   make   not be   not have
not win   see   take

Running
Wild

This week in 'Running Wild', Paula Clifford tells us about her race across the Sahara Desert, in Africa.

'It was great trip, but it **1** .... always fun! I **2** .... the same ten people every day and we **3** .... much time alone.

The desert was beautiful. I **4** .... that it was cold at night and I **5** .... warm clothes with me, but I was always freezing!

Anyway, the experience was amazing and I **6** .... lots of new friends. I **7** .... the race across the desert – I was second – but I learnt a lot about myself.

4 Read the answers. Complete the questions about a famous director, Steven Spielberg.

1 **A:** Where
.... ?
B: Cincinnati, USA.

2 **A:** When
.... ?
B: In 1946.

3 **A:** Where
.... ?
B: At California State University.

4 **A:** When .... a film-maker?
B: He became a film-maker in 1969.

5 **A:** What .... called?
B: His first film was called *The Sugarland Express*.

6 **A:** Why .... an Oscar in 1993?
B: For making *Schindler's List*.

VOCABULARY 1

parts of the body

1 How many have we got? Complete the table with these parts of the body. Use plurals if necessary.

arm back foot hand head leg mouth
neck shoulder toe

one	two	ten
nose	knees	fingers

2 Label the pictures with these words.

face leg foot hand

① ....

② ....

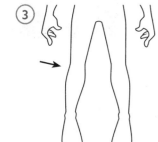
③ ....

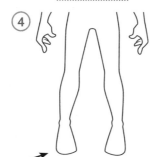
④ ....

3 Look at the photos and write sentences about the people's hair. Use *have got* and these words.

blonde curly dark fair
long short straight wavy

① She's got long curly hair. It's dark.

② ....
....

③ ....
....

④ ....
....

⑤ ....
....

⑥ ....
....

READING

1 Read the article quickly. Are the sentences true (T) or false (F)?

1 Scarlett Johansson is from Los Angeles. ....
2 She started acting when she was a child. ....
3 Scarlett's brother acted in a film. ....
4 Gisele Bündchen's sister is famous. ....
5 The two sisters studied modelling together. ....
6 Gisele liked being tall at school. ....

2 e Read the article again. Choose the correct answer for each gap.

1 **A** on	**B** in	**C** at
2 **A** had	**B** was	**C** got
3 **A** got	**B** get	**C** getting
4 **A** have	**B** has	**C** with
5 **A** the	**B** some	**C** they
6 **A** what	**B** which	**C** that

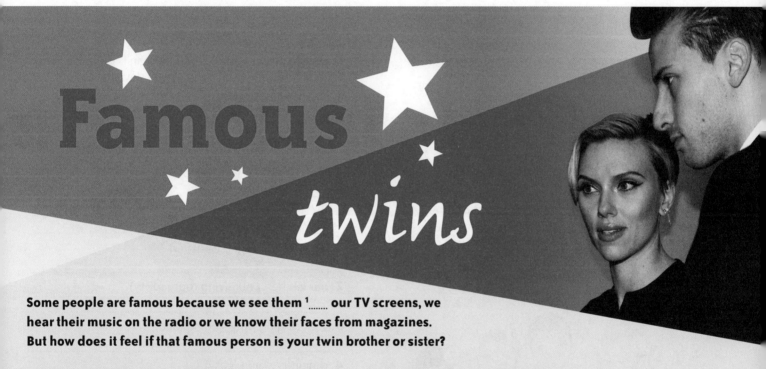

Famous twins

Some people are famous because we see them ¹ .... our TV screens, we hear their music on the radio or we know their faces from magazines. But how does it feel if that famous person is your twin brother or sister?

Acting and politics

Actor Scarlett Johansson is from New York, USA. She acted for the first time in a theatre when she ² .... eight years old. One year later she was in a film. She went to acting school in 2002 and is now famous all over the world for films like *Lost in Translation*, *Iron Man* and the *Captain America* series. But did you know that she has a twin brother called Hunter?

Hunter Johansson has ³ .... brown eyes and dark hair, Scarlett's eyes are green and she's got fair hair. Hunter often goes to 'red carpet' events with Scarlett. Hunter was in one film, with his sister, in 1996 and in a television series in 1981. He is interested in politics and in 2008 he worked with Barack Obama on his presidential campaign.

Working together

Former supermodel Gisele Bündchen ⁴ .... five sisters. Patricia, her twin, is five minutes younger than her famous sister. They grew up in Brazil and they both went to modelling school when they were thirteen years old. She became her sister's manager and spokeswoman. Now ⁵ .... sisters work together at Gisele's clothing company.

Gisele remembers ⁶ .... it wasn't always better to be different. She was much taller and thinner than the other children in her class at school. 'It wasn't fun,' she says.

GRAMMAR

comparative adjectives

1 Read the project and write the names of the people in Wiktor's family.

My family

by Wiktor Jeziorska

Here's a photo of me with my family. You can see my mum, Kasia. She's got long, fair hair. Then there are my two sisters. They are twins, so they look the same, but we always know who is who because Anastasia's hair is longer than Ala's.

That's my uncle, Boris and my dad, Jan. Boris is my dad's younger brother, but he's taller than him.

I've got two cousins. My cousin Dobry is eleven. His hair is short like mine, but it's curlier and fairer. Marek is Dobry's younger brother. They don't look like each other. We all play computer games together and Marek always wins. He thinks it's very funny that we are older, but much worse at computer games than he is.

me

1	5 ....
2	6 ....
3	7 ....
4	

2 Choose the correct words to complete the sentences.

1 My computer is **old / older** than that one.
2 Gill's hair is **curly / curlier** than Jane's.
3 Today is sunnier **than / that** yesterday.
4 The supermarket is **nearer / near** than the market.
5 My picture is **bad / worse** than yours.
6 Scarlett's hair is fairer **then / than** her brother's.

3 Complete the email with the comparative form of the adjectives in brackets.

Hi Ella,

How are you? Is your arm ¹ .... (good) now?

Guess what! We've got a new house! It's ² .... (big) than the old house. It's ³ .... (easy) to find because it's next to the park. The only problem is that my room is ⁴ .... (dark) because of the trees.

This house has got a big garden. Monique loves playing in it. She's ⁵ .... (happy) than she was in the old house. She's four years old now, and she is much ⁶ .... (loud) than before! It's difficult to do my homework these days.

See you soon,

Amanda

4 Write sentences. Use the comparative form of the adjectives in brackets.

my grandfather / my grandmother (old)
My grandfather is older than my grandmother.

1 the book / the film (sad)
....

2 our kitchen / our living room (dirty)
....

3 your singing / my singing (bad)
....

4 running / skiing (easy)
....

5 my school / your school (big)
....

5 Write comparative sentences about you. Use different adjectives.

1 my English / my parents' English
....

2 my bedroom / my parents' bedroom
....

3 my bag / my friend's bag
....

4 my dad / my friend's dad
....

5 my hair / my friend's hair
....

VOCABULARY 2

clothes

1 Choose the correct words to complete the sentences.

1 It's sunny. You need your **sunglasses / tights**.
2 It's cold and windy. I'm wearing my **shorts / jeans**.
3 It's rainy. I've got my **boots / sandals** on.
4 It's cool. Wear your **hoodie / sunhat**.
5 It's hot. I need my **boots / shorts**.
6 It's very cold. Put on a **hat / T-shirt**.

2 Look at the pictures. Complete the crossword.

 ①  ② ③

(4 across)   (4 down)   ⑤

⑥   ⑦

Crossword:
1 across: s h i r t

3 Choose the correct answer, A, B or C.

1 I've got strong .... for walking in the mountains.
   A boots **B** tights **C** sandals
2 I'm going to the beach. Where's my .... ?
   A jeans **B** swimsuit **C** hoodie
3 I forgot my ...., so I can't play tennis.
   A boots **B** sandals **C** trainers
4 We're going to the park. Wear your ....
   A socks **B** jeans **C** swimsuit
5 If I don't wear .... with these shoes, they're too big.
   A shorts **B** socks **C** boots
6 Careful! Don't stand on your ....
   A boots **B** sunglasses **C** shoes
7 Ben doesn't like his new haircut, so he's wearing a .... to hide it.
   A cap **B** skirt **C** shirt
8 Should I wear .... with my blue skirt?
   A shorts **B** tights **C** jeans

4 Complete the blog with these words.

---

boots   jeans   sandals   shirts   shorts   trainers

On Saturdays I help in my parents' clothes shop. We sell men's clothes. At the moment we're selling clothes like **1**_____ and T-shirts because it's summer. But there are also formal **2**_____ and trousers for special occasions. The shop has footwear, too: **3**_____ for going to the beach, shoes and **4**_____ for the winter. We don't sell **5**_____ because we aren't a sports shop. I think the thing we sell every day is **6**_____ . All men wear them because they're blue and they go with everything.

5 Complete the sentences about your clothes.

1 When I meet my friends, I usually wear
   ....
2 My favourite T-shirt is ....
3 I don't have any ....
4 I love wearing ....
5 I don't like wearing ....

LISTENING

1 🔊 **8.1 Listen to a programme about world records and clothes. Match 1–5 with A–E.**

1 first fashion designer
2 longest wedding dress
3 highest shoes
4 most people wearing sunglasses in the dark
5 people who dress the worst in Europe

A India
B Britain
C France
D China
E Spain

2 🄴 🔊 **8.2 Read the notes and try to guess the answers. Listen again and complete the notes.**

Interesting clothes facts

- Rose Bertin made clothes for: the [1] .... of France

- time it took to make the world's longest wedding dress: one [2] ....

- [3] .... cm: the height of the world's highest shoes

- 6 [4] .... 2015: the date 6,774 people wore sunglasses in the dark

- money British people spent on clothes in 2015: [5] .... million euros

superlative adjectives

3 Complete the table.

adjective	superlative
easy	the easiest
slow	[1] ....
big	[2] ....
funny	[3] ....
[4]	the worst
sad	[5] ....
good	[6] ....

4 Rewrite the sentences. Use the opposites of the highlighted words in the superlative form.

My brother's bedroom is the cleanest in the house.
My brother's bedroom is the dirtiest in the house.

1 I think this is the best DVD I've got.

....

2 I've got three cousins. Rafael is the shortest.

....

3 This is the saddest day of my life.

....

4 Our classroom is the hottest in the school.

....

5 They've got three dogs. Pablo is the quietest.

....

5 Complete the sentences with the superlative form of these adjectives.

fast   long   more   small   young

1 The AVE Talgo 350 in Spain is one of the .... trains in Europe. It travels at 330 kilometres per hour.

2 The .... house in Britain is in Conwy, Wales. There are only two rooms – one upstairs and one downstairs.

3 Praia do Cassino in Brazil is the world's .... beach, at 240 km.

4 The .... driver to win the Formula 1 championship was Sebastian Vettel. He was only twenty-three years old when he won.

5 Canada has the .... lakes of all the countries in the world.

SPEAKING

1 Look at the photos (A–F). Where do you think these places are? Match them with the countries.

Austria   Antarctica   Bolivia   Chile   India   the USA

....

....

2 Complete the sentences about the photos in Ex 1.

A Perhaps it's in ..... the USA ..... .

B I think it's ....

C It looks more like ....

D I guess it's ....

E Perhaps it's ....

F I think it's that famous desert in ....

3 🔊 8.3 Listen and check your answers.

4 Match the sentences (1–6) with the photos in Ex 1 (A–F).

1 the highest capital city on Earth   ....

2 the oldest tree in the world   ....

3 the best place to live in the world   ....

4 the driest place on Earth   ....

5 the wettest place on Earth   ....

6 the coldest place on Earth   ....

5 🔊 8.4 Listen, speak and record.

6 🔊 8.5 Listen back and compare.

7 🔊 8.6 Listen and complete the sentences.

1 In .... the temperature in Antarctica is -20°C.

2 The lowest temperature in Antarctica was - .... °C.

3 The driest place on Earth is the Atacama .... in Chile.

4 There are 11,000 millimetres of .... every year in Mawsynram.

5 La Paz is 3,600 metres .... sea level.

6 In ...., experts said that Vienna is the best place to live in the world.

WRITING

1 Complete the sentences with *like, at* or *for*. Write – if the sentences don't need a word.

1 Would you like to look .... the photos from my holiday?

2 Katie doesn't look .... her brother. They are quite different.

3 You look .... nice. Is your hair shorter?

4 Can you help us to look .... the keys?

5 My dad looks .... happy because his back is better.

6 Don't look .... me like that! I don't like it.

7 Look – that cat looks .... Kevin's cat, Rufus.

8 Are you looking .... your laptop? It's on the kitchen table.

2 Rewrite the sentences with the correct punctuation.

daniel says why are you going out

Daniel says, 'Why are you going out?'

1 i need to see grandma says mum

....

2 can i come too asks daniel

....

3 mum says yes thats a good idea

....

4 im going to look for my shoes says daniel

....

5 i think theyre in the kitchen says mum

....

6 yes here they are says daniel

....

3 Look at the pictures. Write a story. Write 20 words or more. Think about these questions.

• Who are the boys?

• What are they doing at home?

• What happens when they go to school?

• How do they look and feel at the end?

UNIT CHECK

1 Match 1–5 with A–E to make clothes words.

1	sun	A	boots
2	T-	B	shorts
3	cycling	C	glasses
4	swim	D	shirt
5	ski	E	suit

2 Label the picture with these words.

arm   finger   hand   head   leg   neck   shoulder

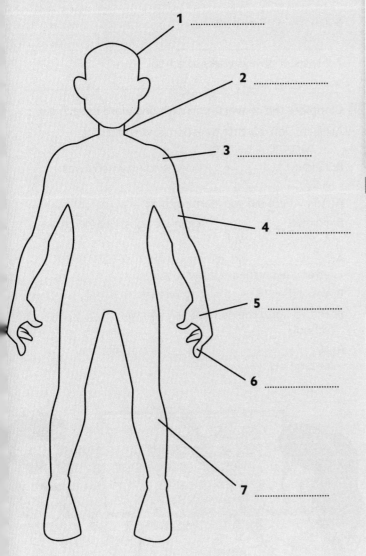

1 ....
2 ....
3 ....
4 ....
5 ....
6 ....
7 ....

3 Draw these things on the picture in Ex 2.

beard   curly hair   eyes   moustache   mouth   nose

4 Choose the correct words to complete the blog.

I am in an Irish dance group and two years ago, we helped to break a **¹world / pop** record. It was very exciting. The record was for the **²more / most** people doing Irish dancing in a line. There were more **³that / than** 2,000 people!

In Irish dancing you need to keep your body and arms very **⁴wavy / straight**, but move your legs and **⁵feet / teeth** quickly. Some dancers wore funny costumes, but I wore my dress, white socks and special shoes. There are two types of shoes for Irish dancing – we used the hard shoes which are much **⁶loudest / louder** than the softer shoes. The soft shoes look **⁷as / like** black ballet shoes.

5 Read the text and write the names under the pictures.

Anna's got the curliest hair. Heidi's hair is the longest. Isobel has got dark, wavy hair. It isn't the shortest hair. Marta's hair is shorter than Jana's and Eva's hair. Eva's mouth is bigger than Jana's mouth.

....

....

REVIEW: UNITS 1–8

1 Write these words in the correct group.

bin   dentist   help   mat   mirror   sing
singer   teach   teacher

things in a room	verbs	jobs

2 Match 1–8 with A–H to make nouns.

1 birthday		**A** whale
2 concert		**B** lesson
3 history		**C** party
4 blue		**D** centre
5 polar		**E** driver
6 shopping		**F** juice
7 apple		**G** bear
8 taxi		**H** tickets

3 Complete the sentences with these prepositions.

above   at   by   for   from   in   on   to

1 All my books are on the shelf .... my bed.

2 My best friend isn't American. He's ....
Brazil.

3 Mother's Day is always .... Sunday
in the UK.

4 I usually go to school .... car.

5 We visited my aunt and uncle ....
the weekend.

6 Don't cross the street .... front of cars.

7 After lunch, we went .... a walk in the park.

8 What time do you usually go .... bed on
Saturdays?

4 Write negative sentences.

My grandma's house has got a garden.
My grandma's house hasn't got a garden.

1 I meet my friends in the evening.

....

2 You must take photos.

....

3 There's some rice in the cupboard.

....

4 We went to a basketball match yesterday.

....

5 She lost her suitcase at the airport.

....

6 I'm having breakfast.

....

7 My sister always walks to school.

....

5 Complete the conversation with one word in each gap.

A: Hello, Don. My first question is: why did you
.......become....... a singer?

B: I did it ¹........................... I loved singing when I was
a boy.

A: And where did you learn to sing?

B: I didn't ²........................... singing lessons. I learned from
³........................... dad.

A: ⁴........................... did you make your first CD? Was it
after you finished school?

B: Yes. When I ⁵........................... twenty.

A: Did you play the guitar when you were ⁶...........................
school?

B: No, I ⁷........................... . I started to play after my
second CD.

6 Write these verbs in the correct group.

climb   play   tidy   travel   wash   write

1	the guitar	football	computer games
2	a mountain	the stairs	trees
3	by car	by plane	by bike
4	your room	the house	the garden
5	the car	the windows	your hair
6	a book	a text message	an email

7 Complete the sentences with the past simple form of the verbs in Ex 6.

1 I .... card games with my grandpa on Sunday.

2 I went walking and .... a big hill at the weekend.

3 My aunt, uncle and cousins .... to London last week.

4 The rain .... all the snow away last night.

5 My teacher .... lots of questions on the board before class.

6 We .... the kitchen after we made a cake.

8 Complete the sentences with one word in each gap.

1 Wednesday is the day after ....

2 A sandwich is two pieces of .... with something inside.

3 Cars, bikes and lorries all have ....

4 .... is the month before June.

5 You can have a .... on the wall to tell the time.

6 A .... is something you walk across over a river.

9 Put the words in the correct order to make questions. Then write short answers about you.

1 in / live / village / you / do / a?

A: ....

B: ....

2 your / is / in / a / classroom / noticeboard / there?

A: ....

B: ....

3 got / your / hair / best / fair / friend / has?

A: ....

B: ....

4 musical / play / you / a / do / instrument?

A: ....

B: ....

5 yesterday / your / go / did / to / parents / work?

A: ....

B: ....

10 Complete the article with one word in each gap.

MOSCOW,
Russia's beautiful capital city

Q: What's the weather ......like...... **in Moscow?**

A: Winter is cold. In fact, the **¹**..................... months in Moscow are January and February, when the temperature is around -9°C. The first snow arrives in October and it stays until April. If you visit in the winter, you **²**..................... wear a warm hat and scarf when you go out.

In summer the temperature is usually around 18°C. The nicest months are July and August, when the temperature **³**..................... be 30°C during the day.

The wettest months are also July and August, with around 90 mm of rain.

Q: When is the best time to visit Moscow?

A: This is a **⁴**..................... question because there is something to see in every season. Maybe the **⁵**..................... time to visit is the beginning of spring or end of autumn, because the weather is very cloudy, cold and rainy. A better time to visit is in the summer or the winter.

79

9 School's out

VOCABULARY 1

sport and activities

1 Complete the definitions with these sports/activities.

dancing   rock climbing   skiing
swimming   tennis   yoga

1 You have to pull yourself up with your hands and arms. ....

2 You usually need music. ....

3 You can play with two or four people. ....

4 You usually need snow. It can be dangerous. ....

5 You can do this in the sea, a lake or a pool. ....

6 You usually need a mat. You can close your eyes. ....

2 Think of three more sports. How would you describe them? Write three sentences.

....

....

....

3 Complete the questions with *play, go* or *do*.

1 Do you .... yoga?

2 How often do you .... swimming?

3 Does your best friend .... basketball?

4 Did you .... surfing last summer?

5 Do any of your friends .... kung fu?

6 Do you .... tennis?

4 Answer the questions in Ex 3.

1 ....

2 ....

3 ....

4 ....

5 ....

6 ....

5 Read the blog post. Choose the correct answer for each gap.

My family has a small boat and in summer I love to go ¹....... in it with my parents. My older sister goes ²....... in the sea, too. She says it's great, but I think it's difficult. We both like to play ³....... on the beach though!

I love my bicycle and I go ⁴....... at the weekends in the countryside. And I sometimes go ⁵....... with my best friend at the park.

At school I play ⁶....... every Tuesday all year. It helps that I'm tall and it's good because you can play it inside or outside.

1 A climbing   **B** sailing   **C** swimming

2 A dancing   **B** surfing   **C** cycling

3 A surfing   **B** camping   **C** volleyball

4 A mountain biking   **B** yoga   **C** dancing

5 A skateboarding   **B** skiing   **C** tennis

6 A baseball   **B** rollerblading   **C** basketball

READING

1 e Read the post and comments. Choose the correct answer.

Which person:	Joe	Patricia	Max
1 is going to be without their parents for a week?	A	B	C
2 is going to stay in a big city?	A	B	C
3 is good at skiing?	A	B	C
4 is going to buy things?	A	B	C
5 is going to be in the quietest place?	A	B	C
6 is going to visit a new place?	A	B	C
7 is going to see lots of relatives?	A	B	C

2 Read the post and comments again. Match these places from the texts with the people.

British Museum   Buckingham Palace   London Eye   Switzerland   train station

1 Joe: ....

2 Patricia: ....

3 Max: ....

3 Which of the places in Ex 2 would you like to visit? Why? Write three sentences.

....

....

....

TWO WEEKS UNTIL THE HOLIDAYS!
What are you going to do this year?

Joe

I'm very excited because I'm going to visit London for the first time with my parents and my two sisters. We're going to see all the famous places –the London Eye, Piccadilly Circus and, of course, Buckingham Palace. I might see the Queen!

My sisters are studying Ancient Egypt at school, so we're going to visit the British Museum and see the mummies.

We're going to see the lights on Oxford Street and do some shopping. I can't wait!

Patricia

London sounds fantastic! I'm not going to be in a big city for the holidays. I'm going to stay in a small town in the mountains in Switzerland and I'm going to ski or snowboard every day. We went to the same place last year, so I'm already good at skiing.

The place is really beautiful. There aren't any cars and during the day it's very quiet. In the evenings, if we aren't too tired, we're going to go dancing or listen to live music in the town. I've got a new snowboard to try. It's going to be amazing!

Max

For the first week of the holidays I'm going to stay with my aunt, uncle and cousins. My parents have to work, so my older brother and I are travelling together without them, on the train. My uncle is going to meet us at the station.

We always have a lot of fun with my cousins. They live in a small town in the countryside, so we all go cycling or walking together. We usually play football matches on my cousin's computer in the evening. This holiday he's going to get a new game. We're always so noisy, it's like a real football competition!

My parents are going to arrive on the twenty-third and then we're going to have a big family party!

GRAMMAR

going to

1 Look at the photos. Write sentences with *going to*.

1 ....
2 ....
3 ....
4 ....
5 ....
6 ....

2 Write negative sentences.

1 We're going to win.

....

2 He's going to sing in the show.

....

3 They're going to have a party.

....

4 I'm going to go camping.

....

5 You're going to clean your bedroom.

....

6 She's going to go cycling.

....

3 Complete the conversation with the correct form of *going to*.

A: Where are you going?

B: To the sports shop in the town centre.

A: What ¹........................ you .... buy?

B: A present for my brother. He ²........................ be fifteen on Friday.

A: What kind of thing does he like?

B: He loves playing tennis, so I ³........................ buy him a new racket.

A: But it ⁴........................ be difficult to choose a racket. What about a T-shirt?

B: No, my parents ⁵........................ get him a T-shirt.

A: Well, let's go and see what they have. I'm good at choosing presents.

B: OK. Let's hurry. We ⁶........................ to be late. The shop closes at 5.30.

4 Make questions. Use *going to*.

1 you / go / to France in the summer?

....

2 you / travel / by plane?

....

3 the weather / be / hot?

....

4 your sister / go / with you?

....

5 you all / stay / in a hotel?

....

6 your dad / try / to speak French?

....

5 Answer the questions about you.

1 Are you going to do any homework tonight?

....

2 Are your grandparents going to visit you at the weekend?

....

3 Are you going to do any sport tomorrow?

....

4 Are your friends going to phone you today?

....

5 Are your parents going to go out tonight?

....

6 Is your mum going to wake you up tomorrow?

....

VOCABULARY 2

health problems

1 Look at the photos and write sentences with these words.

~~a cold~~   a headache   a sore throat   earache
stomachache   toothache

She's got a cold.

2 🔊 9.1 **Listen and choose the correct answer, A, B or C.**

1 She's got a
  A cold.   **B** temperature.   **C** cough.

2 He's got
  A stomachache.   **B** sunburn.   **C** cuts.

3 She's got a
  A temperature.   **B** headache.   **C** sore throat.

4 He's got
  A a headache.   **B** a sore throat.   **C** earache.

5 He's got
  A toothache.   **B** cuts.   **C** a headache.

6 She's got
  A sunburn.   **B** a cold.   **C** toothache.

3 Read the clues and complete the crossword.

```
                    [1]
      [2] m  a  t  t  e  r
                    
                    
                    
            [3]     
      [4]   u     r 
                    
                    
            [5]   u     
                    
              [6]   e   
```

Across

2 You look sad. What's the .... ?

4 I sat in the sun for hours yesterday and I got ....

5 I've got a sore throat and a .... I think it's a cold.

6 I don't feel .... I can't play football today.

Down

1 You've got a .... of thirty-nine degrees! Stay in bed.

3 That's a big .... on your finger.

4 Complete the conversation with one, two or three words in each gap.

A: Hi, Ali. Are ....you OK.... ?

B: No, I feel really hot.

A: [1] .... a temperature?

B: I don't know. But I've got [2] .... throat.

A: Oh dear! Why don't you go and see a [3] .... ?

B: No, I think it's just [4] .... cold.

A: Well, you need [5] .... lots of water.

B: Yes, thanks. I'm going to go to bed early, too.

5 Complete the sentences about your health.

1 I had sunburn when ....

2 When I have a headache, I ....

3 When I have a cold, I ....

4 I sometimes have ....

5 I never have ....

LISTENING

1 🔊 **9.2 Listen to people talking about free time activities. Match the conversations (1–5) with the questions (A–E).**

Which conversation is about:

A a musical instrument? ....

B an after-school club? ....

C a weekend trip? ....

D speaking in public? ....

E a summer holiday? ....

2 ℯ 🔊 **9.3 Listen again and choose the correct answer, A, B or C.**

1 You hear a boy talking to his father. What does Harry want to do?

  A go camping

  B stay in a hotel

  C stay with his grandparents

2 You hear two friends talking about sport. What's the matter with Lily?

  A She doesn't have the right clothes.

  B She wants to stop playing the sport.

  C She doesn't feel well.

3 You hear a teacher talking to a student. Why does Tom need to practise?

  A Parents are going to listen to him.

  B The teacher is going to video him.

  C Italian people are going to listen to him.

4 You hear a mother talking to her daughter. What does Ellen want to be?

  A a music teacher

  B a professional guitarist

  C a pop star

5 You hear a girl talking to her brother. What do they want to take with them?

  A their computer games

  B their MP3 players

  C their mobile phones

like/love + -ing

3 **Complete the sentences with the correct form of these verbs.**

| be | listen | stay | swim | tidy | watch |

1 My cousin wants .... a dancer.

2 I don't like .... my bedroom.

3 Does your friend want .... a film with us?

4 My sister loves .... to music in her room.

5 I don't like .... in the sea.

6 Do you want .... at home this weekend?

4 **Look at James' profile and read the text. Then look at Alex's profile and complete the text about him.**

James Naunton

Age: 14

Loves: computer games

Likes: camping

Dislikes: shopping, classical music

Favourite job: pilot

Dream: visit Africa

James is fourteen. He loves playing computer games and he likes going camping. He doesn't like going shopping or listening to classical music. He wants to be a pilot and he wants to visit Africa one day.

Alex Wakemann

Age: 15

Loves: tennis

Likes: travel

Dislikes: TV, history lessons

Favourite job: photographer

Dream: write a book

Alex is fifteen. He loves __playing__ *tennis and he likes ¹ .... He doesn't like ² .... TV or ³ .... history lessons. He wants ⁴ .... a photographer and he wants ⁵ .... a book one day.*

SPEAKING

1 🔊 9.4 **Listen to Steve and Cam talking about these places. Where are they going to go this afternoon? Tick (✓) the correct photo.**

2 🔊 9.5 **Listen again and answer the questions.**

1 What can you see at the museum?

....

2 Who thinks the exhibition isn't interesting? ....

3 What's the weather like? ....

4 What does Steve need to buy?

....

5 What's the problem on Saturday at the shopping centre? ....

6 How do they find out about the films?

....

3 **Match 1–6 with A–F to make sentences.**

1	How about	**A**	you're right.
2	I'm not	**B**	go shopping.
3	Let's	**C**	about going to see a film?
4	Maybe	**D**	going to the museum?
5	What	**E**	idea.
6	Good	**F**	sure.

4 🔊 9.6 **Look at the photos and make sentences with the words. Record yourself. Listen and check your answers.**

how about

let's

what about

how about

I want to

what about

5 **Complete the conversation with one or two words in each gap.**

A: What are we going to do next weekend?

B: ¹........................... about going camping?

A: I'm not ²........................... . Ben may not want to go. He ³........................... like camping.

B: Hmm … Yes, maybe you're ⁴........................... .

A: How about going surfing at the beach?

B: That's a good ⁵........................... .

A: Great! ⁶........................... get the surfboards out.

WRITING

1 Read the sentences. Are they about yesterday (Y), now (N) or tomorrow (T)?

We're having a great time. .....N.

1 We saw some real dolphins. ....

2 I'm sitting at a restaurant near the sea. ....

3 We're going to try surfing. ....

4 I'm going to have a sailing lesson. ....

5 We went to the top of a very tall building. ....

2 Put the parts of the postcard in the correct order (1–7).

.... Hi Louis,

.... Love, Maggie

.... Tomorrow I'm going to visit the zoo at Casa de Campo. I'm going to see the famous pandas.

.... I'm having a great time in Madrid. Yesterday I went to the Retiro Park and I went on a boat on the lake.

.... I can't wait!

.... See you soon,

.... It was a lot of fun.

3 Complete Karen's notes about her holiday plans with these verbs. You do not need two of the verbs.

go   have   make   meet   play   take   visit   walk

Friday 21 August
morning: **1** .... tennis
afternoon: **2** .... the Roman museum

Saturday 22 August
morning: **3** .... swimming
afternoon: **4** .... Sandra at the beach

Sunday 23 August
morning: **5** .... lunch at Café Bruno
afternoon: **6** .... on the beach with Carla

4 Complete Karen's postcard with the correct form of the verbs in Ex 3.

Saturday 22 July

Dear Mum and Dad,

I'm having a great time in Cornwall. I'm writing this postcard at my breakfast table in the hotel.

Yesterday morning I **1** .... tennis with Carla. I didn't win, but I had a lot of fun.

In the afternoon we **2** .... a museum in the town centre. It was really interesting.

Later this morning I **3** .... swimming and in the afternoon I **4** .... Sandra at the beach. It's sunny today, so this afternoon we're going to play beach volleyball. I can't wait!

Lunch tomorrow is going to be at Café Bruno. I really want **5** .... lunch there because my friends told me the fish is very nice. Then in the afternoon Carla and I **6** .... on the beach.

See you on Monday!

Lots of love,

Karen

5 Look at the photo. Imagine you are on holiday in this place. Write a postcard to your grandparents. Write about something you did and something you are going to do.

Dear Grandma and Grandad,
I'm having a lovely time in … Today we …

UNIT CHECK

1 Complete the sentences with a sport or activity from Unit 9.

When you go cycling in the mountains, it's called
.mountain biking. .

1 When there's snow, people usually go to the mountains to
go ....

2 In .... you hit the ball with your hands.

3 If you need to buy something, you go ....

4 When you're ...., you wear boots with wheels on them.

5 You need a boat to go ....

2 Match the sentences (1–6) with the health problems (A–F).

1 She ate lots of chocolate. ....

2 She did too much singing. ....

3 She stayed in the sun all day. ....

4 She was using a knife. ....

5 She didn't brush her teeth for days. ....

6 She listened to loud music. ....

A She's got sunburn.

B She's got a cut.

C She's got toothache.

D She's got earache.

E She's got a sore throat.

F She's got stomachache.

3 Choose the correct words to complete the sentences.

1 What do you want **doing** / **to do** on holiday?

2 My sister loves *do* / *doing* yoga in
the morning.

3 Francesco and Sergio want **to go** /
going surfing.

4 My brother likes **playing** / **play** basketball.

5 Didn't you want **to play** / **play** football yesterday?

6 My dad doesn't like **go** / **going** shopping with me.

7 The children want **to have** / **having** bigger bedrooms.

4 Complete the sentences with the correct
form of *going to* and these verbs.

be   have   not travel   see   walk   watch

1 My mum .... happy.
I tidied my bedroom!

2 I .... a shower before
I go to the party.

3 We .... by car. The
train is easier.

4 .... you ....
home later?

5 It's raining today, so Carla and her
brother .... TV.

6 He .... a rock
concert on Saturday.

5 Complete the blog with one word in
each gap.

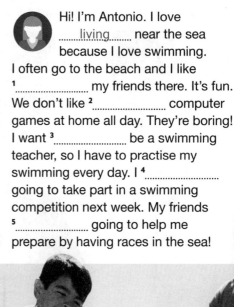

Hi! I'm Antonio. I love
.......living....... near the sea
because I love swimming.
I often go to the beach and I like
¹........................ my friends there. It's fun.
We don't like ²........................ computer
games at home all day. They're boring!
I want ³........................ be a swimming
teacher, so I have to practise my
swimming every day. I ⁴........................
going to take part in a swimming
competition next week. My friends
⁵........................ going to help me
prepare by having races in the sea!

REVIEW: UNITS 1–9

1 Choose the odd one out.

1 doctor	singer	dentist	nurse
2 straight	tall	long	curly
3 boots	sandals	jeans	shoes
4 feet	legs	arms	toes
5 gave	saw	helped	built
6 new	long	short	curly

2 Label the photos with the correct words.

A

B

....

C

D

....

E

F

....

3 Match the sentences (1–6) with the photos in Ex 2 (A–F).

1 You use this to see what you look like. ....

2 It's something you wear on your body to do sport. ....

3 It's a health problem. ....

4 It's someone who does tests and experiments. ....

5 It's something you wear on your feet. ....

6 It's something you send to people when you're on holiday. ....

4 Complete the definitions of these words.

1 cheese   It's a .... made from ....

2 parrot   It's a ....

3 van   You use this to .... on a ....

4 spider   It's an .... with ....

5 nurse   It's ....

6 bridge   You use ....

5 Complete Emma's project with these words.

garden   city   difficult   beautiful   plane
bathroom   upstairs

My family history, by Emma

My great grandmother Betty was born in England. She came to Australia in the 1950s when she was a young woman. Betty grew up in a big **1** .... called Liverpool. I've got some photos of the house but not of the inside. I know it only had one bedroom **2** .... and no **3** .... There was a toilet outside in the **4** ....

Betty's family didn't travel to Australia by **5** .... , they came by ship, so it was a long and **6** .... journey. They moved to a **7** .... house near the sea. It was very different from their life in England. One day I'm going to visit Liverpool and find my great grandmother's house.

6 Read the project again. Change the sentences to make them negative. Use the same verb and tense.

Betty was born in Australia.
Betty wasn't born in Australia.

1 She grew up in London.

....

2 There are some photos of the inside of the house.

....

3 The house had three bedrooms.

....

4 There was a toilet inside the house.

....

5 Betty's family went to Australia by plane.

....

6 Emma is going to visit Sheffield one day.

....

7 Complete the blog with these words in the correct form.

dangerous   good (x2)   interesting   light   quick

Fantastic fencing!

I want to tell you about my new hobby. It's called fencing. You do it indoors and you use a sword. I've got a sword called a foil. It's **1** .... than the swords adults use so younger people can pick it up. The **2** .... sword is the sabre. They're great! I want to learn to use one when I'm older.

Fencing isn't **3** .... – I haven't got any cuts. I wear a special mask to cover my face.

My teacher always says, 'If you want to be **4** .... at fencing, you have to have really **5** .... feet!' I'm trying to get faster every day.

I like watching the other people in the club, too. It's **6** .... and it's a very good way to learn.

I'm going to take part in a competition soon. I'm going to practise a lot at home – without my sword!

8 Put the words in the correct order to make sentences about sport.

1 go / We / in / sometimes / January / skiing

....

2 tall / aren't / players / always / Football

....

3 I / winter / in / like / tennis / really / don't / playing

....

4 rollerblading / playground / the / Don't / in / children's / go

....

5 at / My / sports / usually / basketball / sister / plays / centre / the

....

6 got / swimming / go / temperature / You / when / a / you've / mustn't

....

9 Read the interview with a hockey player. Complete the questions.

A: Hi, Emma. It's lovely to meet you. How **1** .... ?

B: I'm fine, thanks.

A: I'd like to ask about how it all began. When **2** .... playing hockey?

B: I started playing when I was 11.

A: And **3** .... on the school hockey team?

B: No, I wasn't on the team at school. I wasn't very good at first!

A: How **4** .... get better?

B: I played a lot of games and I practised hockey skills in the garden at home.

A: **5** .... being the goalkeeper?

B: Yes, I do. I love it. I think I'm the most important player on the team!

A: What **6** .... at the moment?

B: I'm training for the team's next big competition. It's the Women's Hockey World Cup.

10 Choose the correct answer, A, B or C.

1 What's the date today?
   A It's 14 July.
   B It's Wednesday.
   C On 14 July.

2 When does he have piano lessons?
   A He likes them.
   B Yes, he does.
   C On Friday afternoon.

3 What's your family name?
   A They're Martinez.
   B It's Martinez.
   C I don't know.

4 Can you help me?
   A No, you can't.
   B Yes, of course.
   C Yes, you can.

5 Is there a bus stop near here?
   A Yes, it is.
   B Yes, next to the supermarket.
   C No, thank you.

6 What's the weather like?
   A It's cold.
   B It's like cold.
   C I'm cold.

7 What's the matter?
   A It doesn't matter.
   B It's about health.
   C I've got a headache.

8 How about going camping at the weekend?
   A Yes, I do.
   B Great idea.
   C Yes, I'm going.

READING

1 Write the word that comes before each group. Use these words.

---

have   join   learn   ~~make~~   wear   work

...**make**...	a film	a figure	a sandwich
1	a film school	a club	a group
2	in a group	on a film	at a film school
3	make-up	a costume	a hat
4	fun	a party	an idea
5	to play football	about films	a musical instrument

2 Read the advert and answer the questions.

1 What kind of people do the film-makers need? ....

2 How much do they pay for working in the day? ....

3 What time do the extras have to get to work? ....

4 How many famous actors are working on the film? ....

3 **e** Read the advert. Choose the correct answer for each gap.

1	**A** look	**B** watching	**C** looking
2	**A** in	**B** the	**C** at
3	**A** they	**B** their	**C** them
4	**A** at	**B** up	**C** for
5	**A** never	**B** don't	**C** sometimes
6	**A** you	**B** us	**C** him

Be a **film star!**

Are you aged between eighteen and twenty-five? Do you live in London? Do you want to be in a film? We are **¹**....... for extras for an exciting film project. Extras are people who appear in a film but don't say anything.

Our film takes place in London in the 1800s. Use your acting skills and be part of the drama. We pay £100 a day and £150 when you work **²**....... night. Breakfast and lunch are included.

Extras are very important because **³**....... make our films more real. They usually wear costumes and make-up, just like the stars of the film. Our extras need to get **⁴**....... early – we begin filming at nine o'clock every morning so extras need to arrive at seven thirty. We **⁵**....... work long days when we have to complete a scene, but we also have a lot of fun. Remember, you might see yourself on the big screen when the film is finished!

We can't tell **⁶**....... the name or subject of the film, but we can say that three famous actors are making it with us. Join us and learn all about film-making from real artists – and you never know, in the future, you might be the star! Fill in an application form today.

4 You want to be an extra in the film in Ex 2. Complete the application form.

Film extra application form

Please write your name in BLOCK CAPITALS

First name: **1** ....

Last name: **2** ....

Age: **3** ....

Home city: **4** ....

Home phone number: **5** ....

Email address: **6** ....

---

5 Read the texts. Choose the correct answer, A, B or C.

Hi Clare,
How are you? Is your throat better?
I couldn't tell you at school today, so I'm texting you.
My party is on Saturday afternoon.
Can you come?
Emma x

1 A Clare can't go to the party.
B Clare may be sick.
C Emma wasn't at school today.

Tivoli Gardens Restaurant

Grand opening tomorrow night!
Come and try our new menu.
Free drinks for every table of four people
or more.
Dinner is from 6 p.m. to 10 p.m.

2 How do you get free drinks at the restaurant?
A Take three people with you.
B Try the new menu.
C Arrive before 6 p.m.

Hi Sam,
My brother's got three tickets for a concert tonight.
Are you free? They cost £30 but we only need to pay
him £20. It's at 7.30. Do you want to go?
You need to tell me before 5 p.m.
Ed

3 A Ed wants to know if Sam can go to a concert.
B Ed's brother is going to give him free tickets.
C Ed wants to meet Sam before 5 p.m.

DON'T STOP!
2.30   6.00   8.30
Only children older than twelve can watch this film.

4 A This film is good for very small children.
B You can't watch this film if you are ten.
C Children under twelve can watch this film.

Free to a good home

Beautiful kittens, eight weeks old
Black and white, nice personalities.
We have three adults, so these little ones need
a new home.
Phone Leslie on 077 463 321.

5 Why doesn't Leslie want the kittens?
A Because they aren't very pretty.
B Because they are difficult.
C Because she has three cats already.

Hi!
Shall we go to the sports centre tomorrow?
There is a special volleyball match at 11.30. It's free to
watch and there is food, too. Do you want to meet at
11.15? Let me know.
Dave

6 A Dave wants to play volleyball tomorrow.
B Dave wants to see a volleyball match tomorrow.
C Dave wants to go out for food tomorrow.

10 Films and friends

LISTENING

1 🔊 **10.1 Isobel is an extra on a film. She's making a video diary about her day. Listen and tick (✓) the questions you hear.**

1 What are you eating? ☐
2 Do you like the food here? ☐
3 What time did you start work? ☐
4 Did you travel by car? ☐
5 What's the film about? ☐
6 Why are you waiting? ☐
7 What's the weather like? ☐
8 What's the matter? ☐

2 e 🔊 **10.2 Listen again. Choose the correct answer, A, B or C.**

1 What's the first thing Isobel does after she arrives?
   A She puts on her costume.
   B She has breakfast.
   C She goes to the make-up room.
2 What time did she get up?
   A eight o'clock
   B half past six
   C seven thirty
3 What is Isobel doing in the film?
   A talking to the stars of the film
   B breaking something
   C talking to some friends
4 Where is Isobel waiting?
   A on a beach
   B inside a house
   C on a train
5 Why can't they film?
   A because the film's star has a headache
   B because the cameras aren't ready
   C because the weather is bad

3 🔊 **10.3 Listen again and answer the questions.**

1 When did Karen and Isobel meet?
....
2 When do the film stars start work?
....
3 Why does Yvette love her job?
....
4 What did Isobel see yesterday?
....
5 What's the weather like?
....
6 What day is it tomorrow?
....

4 🔊 **10.4 What is Isobel doing? Write sentences. Use these phrases. Listen again and check your answers.**

get up   go home   have breakfast   have lunch
practise her scene   wait on the beach

▬	6.30	She's getting up.
▬	7.30	1 ....
▬	9.30	2 ....
▬	11.00	3 ....
▬	12.00	4 ....
▬	1.30	5 ....

SPEAKING

1 🔊 **10.5 Listen to two friends talking about films. Tick (✓) the phrases you hear.**

1 I love … ☐
2 My favourite film is … ☐
3 What about you? ☐
4 I'm not sure. ☐
5 Why do you like …? ☐
6 Well, I think they're OK. ☐
7 I don't usually … ☐
8 Really? ☐

2 **Choose the correct answer, A, B or C.**

1 Where do you usually watch films?
   A Yes, I do.   **B** At home.   **C** Not usually.
2 Which type of film do you like best?
   A Movies.   **B** The cinema.   **C** Cartoons.
3 Do you like adventure films?
   A Really?   **B** They're OK.   **C** What about you?
4 What do you think about action films?
   A I'm not sure.   **B** I think so.   **C** Yes, I do.
5 I love films about history.
   A Really?   **B** I love, too.   **C** You're boring.
6 Aren't kung fu films amazing?
   A No, I don't.   **B** It's right.   **C** Yes, they are.

3 🔊 **10.6 Make questions. Record yourself. Listen and check your answers.**

1 animation films / fun
2 action films / interesting
3 romantic films / boring
4 sport films / great
5 animal films / interesting
6 family films / good

> Do you think animation films are fun?

4 **Look at the pictures (1–6) and write your opinion about each type of film. Use *like*, *love*, *don't like* or *think*. Give reasons.**

1 ....
2 ....
3 ....
4 ....
5 ....
6 ....

animal films

action films

cartoons

kung fu films

sport films

3D films

WRITING

1 **Match 1–6 with A–F to make sentences.**

1 I thought it was a   **A** the characters much.

2 I had   **B** this film with my family.

3 I enjoyed this   **C** a good time.

4 I wasn't sure   **D** very good story.

5 I watched   **E** film a lot.

6 I didn't like   **F** about the story.

2 **Rewrite the sentences. Change them from negative to positive or from positive to negative.**

I liked the actors in the film.

I didn't like the actors in the film.

1 I want to read the next book in the series.

....

2 I had a very good time at the concert.

....

3 My sister and I didn't laugh.

....

4 I thought it was an interesting programme.

....

5 My family didn't enjoy watching the film.

....

6 The characters weren't very funny.

....

3 **Read the answers. Complete the questions.**

1 **A:** .... the book about?

   B: It was about some caves in the USA.

2 **A:** .... the main characters?

   B: A girl and her family.

3 **A:** What .... in the end?

   B: The girl went on holiday and found the caves.

4 **A:** .... did .... get the book from?

   B: My grandparents bought it for my birthday.

5 **A:** .... wrote it?

   B: Alexis Rowan.

6 **A:** .... did she write it?

   B: In 2017.

7 **A:** .... did you .... of it?

   B: I enjoyed it. It was very exciting.

4 **Read the reviews and answer the questions.**

> **Gabrielle, 14**   Add message | Report
>
> *Pirate Parrot* is a funny book. It's about a Spanish boy and his pet parrot. The main character, Pablo, thinks that he is a pirate but his parrot doesn't like water. It's a very good story and I laughed a lot when I read it. The writer is a man called Hector Martinez. He worked in a pet shop and that's when he had the idea and he wrote the book. Read it today! You're going to love it, too.

> **Kath, 13**   Add message | Report
>
> I saw an interesting programme last night on TV. It was about the life of a famous Russian dancer. The story started when she was a young child in a village. When she was eleven she won a competition and then she went to study ballet in Saint Petersburg. It was difficult for her when she arrived in the big city but she worked hard and became famous. I enjoyed the programme because I love dancing.

> **Ana, 14**   Add message | Report
>
> On Saturday I went to a concert with my family. The group was called Four Stars. Before the concert I thought they were great but they arrived late and they didn't sing well. They couldn't dance, so the concert was boring. We didn't have a good time. We stayed for an hour and then we went home.

1 What was the name of the group?

....

2 What was the TV programme about?

....

3 Who was the main character in the book?

....

4 Where was the dancer from?

....

5 How long did they stay at the concert?

....

6 Where did the writer of the book work?

....

5 **e** **Complete the review with one word in each gap.**

...........On........... Sunday I saw **¹**........................... amazing TV programme. It was called *Explore Australia* and it was about animals and birds in Australia. We learnt a little about Australia **²**........................... school last year, but I didn't know there were so many interesting animals. There **³**........................... some animals you can't see in any other country in **⁴**........................... world! The presenter took a trip into the desert and she saw camels and red kangaroos there. Then she **⁵**........................... with sharks in the ocean. I thought it was a really interesting programme. I want **⁶**........................... visit Australia now!

Jake, 13

6 **Read the review in Ex 5 again and answer the questions.**

1 When did Jake see the programme?

....

2 What was the title of the programme?

....

3 Why did Jake already know something about Australia?

....

4 What did the presenter see in the desert?

....

5 Which type of fish did she see?

....

6 What does Jake want to do, after watching the programme?

....

7 Write a review of a book, concert or TV programme. It can be real or imaginary. Make notes first. Think about these questions.

- What was it called?
- What was it about?
- What happened?
- Did you enjoy it? Why/Why not?

AUDIOSCRIPTS

S.1

Here's a photo of my family. Our name is Holman. This nice lady is my grandma. Her name is Lily. She's sixty-five years old now. Here's my dad, Tim, and my mum, Ellen. He's thirty-eight and she's thirty-four. They're from London. My cat is there too, can you see? His name is Fluffy. He's thirteen now. That's very old for a cat!

And that's my brother. His name is Alex and he's fourteen. He's with my cousin. Her name is Jenny. She's eleven like me. And that's Jenny's mum. My aunt's name is Jill. She's my dad's sister. She's forty-one, I think. My uncle's name is Charlie. He's forty-nine years old. There's a big party for his birthday next week!

S.2

1 Can you spell 'March'?
2 Can you spell 'July'?
3 Can you spell 'April'?
4 Can you spell 'October'?
5 Can you spell 'January'?
6 Can you spell 'September'?
7 Can you spell 'December'?
8 Can you spell 'February'?

S.3

1 M–A–R–C–H
2 J–U–L–Y
3 A–P–R–I–L
4 O–C–T–O–B–E–R
5 J–A–N–U–A–R–Y
6 S–E–P–T–E–M–B–E–R
7 D–E–C–E–M–B–E–R
8 F–E–B–R–U–A–R–Y

S.4

A: Oh look! It's all about Harry Styles. He's my favourite singer.
B: Me too. I think I know everything about Harry already.
A: OK. Here's a test for you. What's Harry's second name?
B: It's Edward. E–D–W–A–R–D.
A: Yes, it is. When's his birthday?
B: His birthday? Wait a moment … It's the first of January. No, it isn't. It's the first of February.
A: Yes. Right again! Where is he from?
B: That's easy. He's from England.
A: Yes, but where in England?
B: I think he's from Cheshire. Is it C–H–E–S–H–I–R–E?
A: Yes, it is! Well done! What about his family? What's his sister's name?

B: His sister's name is Gemma. G–E–M–M–A. And his step-brother's name is Mike.
A: Wow! You're an expert. What about Harry's first pop group at school? Do you know its name?
B: Yes! White Eskimo.
A: Fantastic! And the last question: What's Harry's favourite football team?
B: Is it Liverpool?
A: No. It's Manchester United!

1.1 and 1.2

M = Mum G = Girl B = Boy

1
M: Look at these. Which one do you like?
G: This apartment is the same as our apartment. It's got a garage.
M: Yes, it's got a garage, but I don't like it. I like houses with gardens. Our apartment hasn't got a garden.
B: Oh! Can we live in a house, please?
M: OK. We can look at some houses.

2
G: I want to live in a house, too. Sam can play in the garden. Let's get a house!
M: Yes, that's right, he can. Dogs love gardens.
G: Poor Sam. He sits on the balcony all the time.
B: Yes, he doesn't like the balcony. He wants to be outside!

3
M: Look! This house has got three bedrooms.
B: Hooray! I can have a bedroom. Our apartment has got two bedrooms and I'm always with Helen.
G: Yes, I don't like our bedroom. It's got two beds and no space for toys.
M: OK. Our new house needs three bedrooms, not two.

4
M: The house is nice, but it isn't near the school.
G: Where is it?
M: It's near the shops.
B: That's OK. We can get the bus to school.
M: Hmm … Maybe.

5
M: OK. I need to call the estate agent. Let's see … What's the name in the paper?
B: It's Brents. B–R–E–N–T–S.
M: Let's call and we can see the house on Saturday.
G: On Saturday? Can we come too, Mum?
M: Yes, of course you can!

1.6

1
A: What's your mobile number, Jill?
B: It's 07781 432 987.
A: Can I read that back to you? 07781 432 987.
B: Yes, that's right.

2
A: My new number at work is 01184 960 325.
B: 01184 960 325. Is that right, Mum?
A: Yes.

3
A: Greg, have I got the right number for you? I've got 07700 900 784.
B: 07700 900 784? Yes, you've got the right number.
A: Great!

4
A: What's your phone number, Skye?
B: It's 01514 960 591.
A: Can I read that back to you? 01514 960 595.
B: No, the last number is 1. 0591.
A: OK. Got it, thanks.

5
A: Todd, is this your number: 02090 180 672?
B: Yes, my number is 02090 180 672.
A: Thanks.

6
A: My new mobile number is 07700 900 162.
B: 07700 900 162?
A: Yes, that's right.
B: Thank you, Pablo.

2.1 and 2.2

R = Rob D = Dillon

R: Hi, Rob. How are you? What's that?
D: It's my 'Walk to School' badge.
R: Why do you have a 'Walk to School' badge?
D: Because it's 'Walk to School' month.
R: Do you mean this October?
D: Yes. In October we walk to school in the morning in a group. We meet in the park at eight o'clock in the morning.
R: Eight o'clock! Why do you do that?
D: It's good to do exercise and it's fun!
R: Do you get a badge every day?
D: No, we get the badge at the end of the month.
R: Do you walk with your mum and dad?
D: No, we walk with my friend's mum. Her name's Mrs Greenhow.

R: G–R–E–E–N–H–O–W? I know her! She's my sister's teacher!

D: Well, she's the leader of the 'Walk to School' group, too.

R: And do your mum and dad walk to work in October, too?

D: Dad doesn't. He goes to work on the train. But mum walks with us on parents' day. That's on Monday morning.

R: What's on the badge? Can I see?

D: It's a star. Look! The picture is different every month.

R: That's really nice. I'm going now – my school starts in ten minutes!

D: Oh no! It's 'Run to School' time!

2.3–2.5

1 It's nine o'clock.
2 It's ten thirty. It's half past ten.
3 It's twelve fifteen.
4 It's two forty-five.
5 It's four o'clock.
6 It's nine thirty. It's half past nine.

2.6

This is the timetable at my new school. The day starts at eight forty-five. Lessons start at nine o'clock. We have a break at half past ten in the morning. Lunch starts at half past twelve. We have an hour. Afternoon break is at two forty-five. Then we have the last lesson of the day. We go home at four o'clock. My favourite lessons are sport and science. We have sport on Monday morning. Science is on Tuesday in the afternoon.

3.1 and 3.2

J = Jake   M = Mum   L = Laura

J: Is this the brochure for the tour in Peru?

M: Yes, it is. There are lots of animals and birds to see.

L: Which birds do we see? Can I have a look? When do we leave?

M: The tour starts in December, Laura. … Let's see. Day 1: we drive from Cusco up to the mountains to begin our seven-day tour. The views are great and we can see our first animals.

J: What do we see? Is it snakes?

M: No, not snakes, Jake. Monkeys!

L: I can't wait!

L: What about the second day?

M: Let's see … On day 2 we go to the river and take a boat trip. We usually see Caiman here.

L: What are Caiman? Are they frogs?

M: No, Caiman are a type of crocodile. They live in rivers and streams and they like sitting in the sun. So they are very easy to see.

L: Are they dangerous?

M: Um … no. The brochure says Caiman never attack people because they are too small. They eat jungle animals.

M: Ah! Laura, listen to the description of day 3. In the morning we visit Blanquillo, where we often see macaws and parrots. They fly in large groups and eat clay.

L: Hooray! I love parrots. They're my favourite birds.

J: What about snakes?

M: Er … no, not on day 3.

J: Where do we go in the afternoon?

M: Um … we go to Camungo Lake.

J: And what is there at the lake? Are there any dolphins?

M: Not dolphins. I think there are river dolphins in South America, but they don't usually live in lakes.

J: So what is there at the lake?

M: There are lots of different birds like quetzals. Um … oh! It says, 'On day 4 in the evening we walk around the lake to find interesting frogs.'

J: That sounds like fun. Frogs always come out in the dark.

M: Yes, it says that the evening is the best time to see them. And they make lots of noise!

J: Does it talk about snakes? I love snakes!

L: Yuk! Why do you like snakes? They're dangerous.

J: I don't know, but I really want to see one.

M: Well, here we are: day 5: we go on a walk through the forest. This is often a good place to see snakes like the Green Tree Viper.

J: Great!

M: And on day six of the tour we go back to Cusco by bus.

L: What animals and birds do we see?

M: From the bus we usually see butterflies and hummingbirds.

J: Oh! We're learning about hummingbirds at school.

M: What do you know about hummingbirds, Jake?

J: Um … they're very small and they usually drink from flowers. And they're very beautiful. I really want to see a hummingbird, too!

3.6

1 Where does this animal live?
2 What does it eat?
3 Has it got legs?
4 Does it swim?
5 How long is it?
6 Is it a snake?

4.1

A: Erik, can you tell me about how your family travels around? What kind of vehicles have you got at home?

B: Well, I've got a bike. It's red and it's a mountain bike. I usually cycle at the weekend with my friends.

A: That sounds nice. What about your parents?

B: They've got two cars. My dad's got a small, black car for going to work and my mum's got a big, family car. We go to school by car every day with my mum.

A: What about your sister?

B: Flavia? She's learning to drive but she hasn't got a car. She usually goes to university by bus. It's on the other side of the city.

A: Has anyone in your family got a motorbike?

B: No, but my uncle's got a lorry! He helps people to move house, so it's usually full of chairs, tables and things.

A: Do your grandparents live near you?

B: Yes, they do. They can walk to our house, so I see them nearly every day.

4.2 and 4.3

A: Would you like to colour the picture?

B: Yes, please.

A: Can you see the curtains in the window of the café?

B: Yes, I can.

A: Colour them red.

B: OK, red curtains.

A: Now I'd like you to colour the bike.

B: The woman's bike?

A: Yes, please. Use your favourite colour. What's that?

B: My favourite colour? Um … blue.

A: OK, that's nice. A blue bike.

B: I like that colour.

B: Can I do some writing?

A: Yes, I'd like you to write 'Coffee Time'.

B: Where?

A: On the sign above the café.

B: Coffee Time. OK.

A: Can you see the dog?

B: No, I can't.

A: It's under the man's table, at the café.

B: Oh yes! I can see it now.

A: Please colour it yellow.

B: Can I colour the train now?

A: Yes, you can. That's a very good idea.

B: What colour?

A: Make it green, please.

B: OK. Where is the train going?

A: To Madrid.

AUDIOSCRIPTS

4.4 and 4.5

1
A: Where would you like to go?
B: I'd like to go to the sports centre.
A: Why?
B: Because there's basketball today.
A: Great idea. Let's go!

2
A: I want to go to the cinema this evening because there's a new film.
B: Can I come too?
A: Of course.

3
A: I'd like to go to the museum next.
B: Why?
A: Because it's got my favourite painting in it.
B: OK.

4
A: I want to go to the shops because I need a book for geography.
B: Oh? What's it about?
A: The USA.

5
A: Where would you like to go today?
B: I'd like to go to the supermarket.
A: Why?
B: Because I want some food!
A: OK!

6
A: I'd like to go to the park this morning.
B: Are you going to ride your new bike?
A: Yes. I want to cycle.
B: Have a good time.

4.6

1 Excuse me. Where's the train station, please?
2 Excuse me. Where are the toilets, please?

4.7

1 bus stop
2 park
3 shopping centre
4 souvenir shops
5 square
6 taxis

4.8

1 Excuse me. Where's the bus stop, please?
2 Excuse me. Where's the park, please?
3 Excuse me. Where's the shopping centre, please?
4 Excuse me. Where are the souvenir shops, please?
5 Excuse me. Where's the square, please?
6 Excuse me. Where are the taxis, please?

5.1

A: Hi, Thais! How are you?
B: Hi, Jessica! I'm fine, thanks. It's lovely to speak to you. What's the weather like in London?
A: Oh, it's very cold and it's raining. I'm staying inside.
B: It's raining here too.
A: Raining? But isn't it summer in São Paulo?
B: Yes, I know. It *is* summer for us. It's very hot. Summer starts in December. But it always rains a lot in summer.
A: I see. So when does it stop raining?
B: Well, in autumn it's cloudy but there isn't so much rain. That's April and May. And in winter it doesn't rain much at all.
A: I think it's so strange that winter for you is June, July and August! That's when I go on my holidays!
B: Yeah! It's winter but it isn't cold – maybe twenty-four degrees. You can still go on holiday in winter in Brazil. Or maybe in spring. That's when it's very sunny and warm – in September, October and November.
A: Oh … I'd really like to come and visit one day. I'd love to go to the beach on Christmas day!
B: Yes. Please come and visit me one day! And I'd like to wake up on Christmas morning when it's snowing!

5.2 and 5.3

A: Hi, Ellen.
B: Hi! This is great! I can't wait for the band to start. I hope it doesn't rain, though.
A: Yeah. It's cloudy again. … Look, there's Lucy!
B: Lucy? Where?
A: Right at the front. She's got her mobile phone in the air.
B: Oh yes. She's videoing the band before the music starts!
A: Who's your favourite member of the band?
B: Nick.
A: Which one is Nick?
B: The one with the cap on.
A: The one playing the drums?
B: Yes. That's Nick.
A: I can see Alice now, too.
B: Alice? Where is she?
A: She's carrying her guitar. Can you see her?
B: Oh yes, I see her now. … Is she the singer?
A: No, she isn't. She never sings.
A: Who's the singer, then?
B: Mark, of course! Really! Don't you know anything?

A: Who's Mark? The one drinking water?
B: No. Mark's the one reading. He doesn't play any instruments. He just sings. He's reading because he's got a lot of words to remember.
A: Right.
A: Who's that girl over there?
B: The one eating a sandwich?
A: Yes, the one next to Lucy. Is she her sister?
B: No, she's her cousin. Her name's May.
A: There are lots of people arriving now, look.
B: Yes. I'm glad we've got a good view. What about your friend Tom? Is he here?
A: Yes, there he is. He's eating a banana.
B: Oh yes. Tom's always hungry.
A: Here we go … The music's starting …
B: And so is the rain … oh no!

5.4

A: Well, I can see one difference.
B: What is it?
A: The … um … how do you say this in English?
B: Shop. Oh yes, I see. In picture A it's a bookshop.
A: And in picture B it's a sports shop.
B: Great. What about the garden near the house? Are there any flowers in picture B?
A: Yes. How many are there? Let's see … Six.
B: OK. That's another difference. There are five flowers in picture A.
A: Fantastic. Last difference …
B: It's the weather. Look! It's … What's the English for this weather?
A: Cloudy.
B: Oh, yes. Thanks. It's cloudy in picture A but it's sunny in picture B.
A: Yay! Finished.

5.5

1 What has the woman got in her hand?
2 What's the weather like?
3 How many girls are there?
4 What is the man doing?
5 How many flowers are there?
6 What is there on the girl's bag?

6.1

Saturday is my favourite day of the week. I usually get up at seven o'clock and I wash my hair. I have breakfast and then I help my dad at the market. The market is in the town centre. I love it in the morning because the streets are closed to cars and it's really quiet. We arrive at eight o'clock and set up our stall. It's a clothes stall. I stay at the market with my dad all morning. It's fun because people talk to us and my friends usually visit me. When the market is finished, around lunchtime, we clean the street. In the afternoon I go to the cinema or the sports centre with my friends.

6.2

1 Last weekend we stayed with my grandma. She's from York, in the north of England. On Saturday afternoon we visited a really good museum. It's called the Jorvik Viking Centre. I was surprised when we arrived because the museum isn't in an old building. It's in a shopping centre!

2 The first thing you see at the museum is the Viking part of the city – through a window under your feet! It was very interesting. There was a brilliant ride called the Time Machine. The Time Machine was a little train and my grandma, my sister and I were inside. It was fun.

3 In the Time Machine train there was a real computer. It helped us to understand the things that we could see. I loved it! There were six different languages to choose from. The Time Machine train travelled past Vikings who were near the river and they talked to us! Then it visited a farm.

4 The thing I liked a lot was the way the Time Machine train showed real people. There was a Viking market, which was loud and dirty. And there was a family in their house, singing and eating. We learned about typical Viking food. They didn't eat much fruit. They usually had fish and meat with bread.

5 The last thing on the Time Machine ride is a big house and you see the bedroom. There was a beautiful bear skin on the bed. And in the garden of the house was a real Viking toilet! It was a really interesting day and we learned a lot.

7.1 and 7.2

A: What are you writing about for the homework, Bruno?

B: I'm writing about when I went to Milan in 2017.

A: Milan? Where's that?

B: It's in Italy.

A: Why did you go to Milan?

B: There was a special event there for people who love building. I went with my sister and my parents. We built a really tall tower out of plastic bricks.

A: How did you do that?

B: Well, we didn't build it by ourselves! About eighteen thousand people built it. We wanted to break the record for the tallest tower made of toy bricks in the world. People in different countries try to build the biggest tower – in 2008 they built a tower in England and before that it was in 2007 in Canada.

A: And how tall was the tower in Italy?

B: It was thirty-five metres tall in the end.

A: That's a lot of bricks!

B: Yes, about five hundred and fifty thousand bricks.

A: Wow! Where did they all come from?

B: They always use the same bricks in each country that builds a tower. They always come from Denmark.

A: And how long did people work on the tower?

B: Five days. They started building on the seventeenth of June and finished on the twenty-first of June.

A: That's amazing!

B: Yes. And a famous Italian TV presenter put the last brick on top of the tower.

A: Did he?

B: Yes, his name was Alessandro Cattelan. C–A–T–T–E–L–A–N.

A: What happened when they finished the tower? Did they leave it there?

B: No, the tower isn't there now. They took the bricks back to Denmark. But the company who make the bricks gave money to a charity afterwards.

A: Great idea. How much money did they make?

B: Umm, they gave seven euros for every centimetre of the tower, so … I can't do the maths! A lot of money!

A: It sounds great. So that's what you're writing about for 'The trip that changed your life'. Why did it change your life?

B: Yes. It was a really good experience. When I saw the finished tower, I thought that all the small things we do are important. My family and I learnt to work with other people and together. And we made some new friends.

A: Wow! I need to think hard about what to write now!

7.3

Ben went on holiday. It was cold when he left home. He went with his mum, dad and brother. They went to the airport and waited for three hours. It was boring. But when they saw a famous tennis player called Alex Bravo, they were very excited. Next Ben found the tennis player's sunglasses on the floor. In the end, Alex Bravo gave his sunglasses to Ben. Ben said, 'Thank you very much!' He was very happy.

8.1 and 8.2

I = Interviewer   E = Ellen

I: We're very happy to welcome Ellen Prince to our programme today. She works for the new fashion museum and she's going to tell us some interesting facts about clothes. Ellen, over to you.

E: Well, my first clothes fact is about the world's first fashion designer. Her name was Rose Bertin and she lived about three hundred years ago in France. One of her most famous clients was Marie Antoinette, the queen of France. She made some really amazing dresses!

And here is another amazing dress. The wedding dress with the longest train in the world. The train is the part of the dress at the back which goes on the floor when the bride walks. This dress was made in China in 2017. It took twenty-two people one month to make it.

A pair of shoes also broke another record. They are the highest shoes in the world, at ninety-four centimetres. A man called James Syiemiong made them in India. But can anyone walk in them?

There are some crazier records. Did you know that there is a record for the most people wearing sunglasses in the dark? On the sixth of September 2015, six thousand seven hundred and seventy-four people got together in Valladolid, Spain, to set this record. They all had to wear their sunglasses in the dark for five minutes. It was ten o'clock at night!

And I'm afraid that people say the British are the people who dress the worst in Europe. Forty-four percent of Europeans who answered a recent survey thought that British people dress worse than them. And this is strange because British people spend the most on clothes – in 2015 it was seventy million euros!

8.3

A

A: Where do you think this tree is? It looks very old.

B: Yes, it's amazing. Perhaps it's in the USA.

A: Let's check the answer key … Yes, it is!

B

A: This is a beautiful photo, but I don't know if I want to go there.

B: Hmm … too cold. I think it's Antarctica.

A: Yes, you're right.

C

A: Do you think this is Africa?

B: No, it looks more like India.

A: Yes, maybe it is. Let's see … Yes, it's India.

AUDIOSCRIPTS

D

A: This looks like South America. I guess it's Chile.

B: No, it isn't. It's Bolivia. It's the capital city, La Paz.

E

A: Is this a photo of Berlin?

B: No, it looks smaller than Berlin. Perhaps it's Vienna.

A: Let's see … You're right again! It's Vienna, in Austria.

F

A: Maybe this photo is Bolivia as well.

B: I don't think so. I think it's that famous desert in Chile.

A: Umm … That's correct!

8.4 and 8.5

1 Maybe it's the highest capital city on Earth.

2 I think it's the oldest tree in the world.

3 I think it's the best place to live in the world.

4 Perhaps it's the driest place on Earth.

5 Perhaps it's the wettest place on Earth.

6 I guess it's the coldest place on Earth.

8.6

A: Hello and welcome to *Where on Earth?* In today's programme we're going to hear some very interesting facts about places all over the world. Where is the coldest place on Earth? Where is the highest capital city? And, perhaps the question we all want to know the answer to: where is the best place to live in the whole world? To answer those questions, we have Professor Green from the World Record Association. Welcome to the programme, Professor Green.

B: Thank you. It's great to be here.

A: Well, can we start by talking about the weather? I think that Antarctica is the coldest place on Earth. Am I right?

B: Yes, you are. Antarctica is the coldest continent. Even in summer, the temperature in higher parts of Antarctica is around minus twenty. But the lowest temperature recorded there was minus eighty-nine degrees Celsius. That's eighty-nine degrees below zero.

A: And from the coldest place to the driest. Perhaps it's the Sahara Desert in Africa?

B: No, it isn't in Africa. It's actually in South America. The Atacama Desert in Chile has less than one millimetre of rain per year.

A: Wow! I didn't know that.

B: Yes, most people think it's the Sahara. And what about the wettest place in the world? Do you know where it is?

A: I guess it's the Amazon rainforest. Is that right?

B: Wrong again! The wettest place on Earth is in India and it's called Mawsynram. There are around eleven thousand millimetres of rain there every year.

A: Eleven thousand! Wow! I don't know if I want to live there.

B: Perhaps you'd like to live in the highest capital city in the world: La Paz in Bolivia. This amazing city is three thousand six hundred metres above sea level.

A: Maybe. But where do experts say is the best place in the world to live?

B: Perhaps this will surprise you. It's Vienna in Austria. In a survey in 2015, experts discovered that people who live there had the best quality of life.

A: Well, that's another thing I didn't know! Thank you very much, Professor, for joining us today.

B: You're welcome.

A: Next on the programme we're going to …

9.1

1

A: What's the matter?

B: I don't know. I'm very tired and I feel really hot.

2

A: Are you OK?

B: Not really. It's my stomach – I don't feel well and I can't eat.

3

A: I can't hear you. What's the matter?

B: I can't speak very well.

4

A: I don't feel well.

B: Why? What's the matter?

A: It's my ears. I think I need to see a doctor.

5

A: What happened to you?

B: I fell over, look at my knees.

A: Oh dear! They look sore.

6

A: I don't want any lunch today.

B: Why not?

A: It's my teeth. I need to go to the dentist's.

9.2 and 9.3

1

A: Your mother and I are thinking about the holiday in August. Do you want to stay in a hotel again this year, Harry?

B: I didn't like being at the hotel last year. It was really noisy. I like staying in the flat with Grandma and Grandpa.

A: Are you sure? Do you want to try camping, maybe?

B: No, thanks. It's going to be too hot to go camping. And if we stay with Grandma and Grandpa, we can swim in their pool every day.

2

A: Are you OK, Lily? Have you got your shorts and trainers?

B: Yes, I have. But I don't want to play today.

A: Why? Do you feel OK?

B: I'm fine. It's just that I don't like playing basketball any more. I want to swap to the after-school tennis club.

3

A: Here's your homework, Tom. It's very good. Now you need to read it to me.

B: But I don't like speaking in front people.

A: That's why it's important to practise. I know there are going to be lots of parents listening, but remember that they all want you to do well. And I'm sure they all like hearing about Italian art.

4

A: How was your guitar lesson?

B: It was good, thanks. I like using the new book …

A: … But you don't like practising! Ellen, I know it isn't easy, but don't you want to be a pop star?

B: Not a pop star, Mum, a classical guitarist. And I know: 'if I want to be a guitarist one day, I have to practise every day'. OK, Mum!

5

A: Are you ready? Dad says we need to finish packing tonight. That way we can leave early tomorrow and have all weekend away.

B: I'm almost ready. I really want to pack my phone!

A: I know! So do I, but we can't. Mum and Dad don't like taking gadgets when we go camping. They want us to relax and enjoy nature. No loud music, no phone calls.

B: I don't want to play music. I'm leaving my MP3 player at home. But I love playing on my phone.

9.4 and 9.5

A: How about going to the museum this afternoon, Cam? There's a new exhibition about the history of sports.

B: I'm not sure. My sister said it's not that interesting.

A: But it's raining. What can we do?

B: Let's go shopping. I need some boots.

A: No, sorry. I really don't like shopping. And on Saturday there are always lots of people at the shopping centre.

B: Maybe you're right. What about going to see a film?

A: Yeah, good idea. We can go online and see what's on.

9.6

1 How about having a party?
2 Let's go swimming.
3 What about playing baseball?
4 How about going cycling?
5 I want to play tennis.
6 What about doing yoga?

10.1–10.4

I = Isobel   K = Karen   Y = Yvette

I: Hi! I'm Isobel and this is my video diary about being an extra. This is my first film and I'm having a lot of fun. We're on location in the countryside. It's half past seven in the morning and I'm eating breakfast! I always eat before I go to the make-up room and put on my costume, because I know it's going to be a long day. I'm having a hot meal with some tea and talking to the other extras. This is my friend, Karen. We started work together last month.

K: Hi!

I: Karen, do you like the food here?

K: Yes, I do! It's delicious.

I: Hello again. It's eight o'clock now and I'm in the make-up room. This lovely woman is called Yvette and she is helping to make me look beautiful. It's not easy because I got up at six thirty this morning! There are big, grey circles under my eyes. Yvette, what time did you start work?

Y: I started at half past seven. I did the stars' make-up first. They start work before the extras, you know.

I: Do you enjoy your job, Yvette?

Y: Yes, I love it because it's never boring. I work on lots of different films.

I: It's half past nine. We're practising for the big scene later. In the film I'm going to be talking with some friends. We have to practise talking quietly because the stars of the film are talking at the same time. We're having a break at the moment. We can talk loudly for a while! There's my friend, Karen. … Karen, tell me, what's the film about?

K: We don't know the story! The makers of the film don't want to tell us because it's a secret.

I: It's eleven o'clock now. We're all waiting for filming to start. I like working near the sea. It's better than being inside. Yesterday I saw some dolphins! But waiting is the one bad thing about being an extra. There's a lot of waiting. Once I had to wait for five hours on a train. I don't know what the problem is today. I'm listening to some music while I wait on the beach, and talking to you on my video diary!

I: Hello again! It's half past one in the afternoon now. We aren't waiting any more but we didn't film the scene. They didn't even start the cameras! We had lunch at twelve and then we waited and waited – it's a real headache! Karen, tell us, what's the weather like?

K: Well, Isobel, it's not very nice! It's cloudy and it's raining. No more filming today.

I: Yes, that's right. We're going home. We're not going to work tomorrow because it's Sunday. But on Monday we start all over again. Just another day in the life of an extra. Bye, everyone!

10.5

A: What's your favourite type of film?

B: I love funny films. What about you?

A: Hmm … I like funny films but I'm not sure they are my favourite.

B: Do you like action films?

A: Well, I think they're OK. I think I like animal films best.

B: Really? Why?

A: Because I think the stories are interesting. And my little brother can watch them, too. They're family films.

10.6

1 Do you think animation films are fun?
2 Do you think action films are interesting?
3 Do you think romantic films are boring?
4 Do you think sport films are great?
5 Do you think animal films are interesting?
6 Do you think family films are good?

IRREGULAR VERBS LIST

Verb	Past simple	Past participle
be	was/were	been
become	became	become
begin	began	begun
bring	brought	brought
build	built	built
buy	bought	bought
catch	caught	caught
choose	chose	chosen
come	came	come
cost	cost	cost
cut	cut	cut
do	did	done
draw	drew	drawn
drink	drank	drunk
drive	drove	driven
eat	ate	eaten
fall	fell	fallen
feed	fed	fed
feel	felt	felt
fight	fought	fought
find	found	found
fly	flew	flown
forget	forgot	forgotten
get	got	got
give	gave	given
go	went	gone/been
have	had	had
hear	heard	heard
keep	kept	kept
know	knew	known
learn	learnt/learned	learnt/learned
leave	left	left
let	let	let

Verb	Past simple	Past participle
lose	lost	lost
make	made	made
mean	meant	meant
meet	met	met
pay	paid	paid
put	put	put
read	read	read
ride	rode	ridden
ring	rang	rung
run	ran	run
say	said	said
see	saw	seen
sell	sold	sold
send	sent	sent
show	showed	shown
shut	shut	shut
sit	sat	sat
sleep	slept	slept
speak	spoke	spoken
spend	spent	spent
stand	stood	stood
steal	stole	stolen
swim	swam	swum
take	took	taken
teach	taught	taught
tell	told	told
think	thought	thought
understand	understood	understood
wake	woke	woken
wear	wore	worn
win	won	won
write	wrote	written

Grammatical Key

adj adjective
adv adverb
conj conjunction
det determiner
dis discourse marker
excl exclamation
int interrogative
n noun
poss possessive
prep preposition
pron pronoun
v verb

A

above *prep*
address *n*
afraid *adj*
after *prep*
age *n*
all *adj + adv + det + pron*
all right *adj + adv*
along *prep*
always *adv*
another *det + pron*
any *det + pron*
app *n*
around *prep*
asleep *adj*
at *prep of time*
aunt *n*
awake *adj*

B

back *adj + adv + n*
bad *adj*
badly *adv*
balcony *n*
band (music) *n*
basement *n*
bat *n*
be called *v*
beard *n*
because *conj*
before *prep*
below *prep*
best *adj + adv*

better *adj + adv*
blanket *n*
blond(e) *adj*
boring *adj*
both *det + pron*
bottle *n*
bottom *adj + n*
bowl *n*
brave *adj*
break *n*
brilliant *adj*
Brilliant! *excl*
bring *v*
build *v*
building *n*
bus station *n*
bus stop *n*
busy *adj*
buy *v*
by *prep*

C

café *n*
cage *n*
call *v*
car park *n*
careful *adj*
carefully *adv*
carry *v*
catch (e.g. a bus) *v*
CD *n*
centre (US center) *n*
change *v*
cheese *n*
cinema *n*
circle *n*
circus *n*
city *n*
city/town centre
(US center) *n*
clever *adj*
climb *v*
cloud *n*
cloudy *adj*
clown *n*
coat *n*

coffee *n*
cold *adj + n*
come on! *excl*
comic *n*
comic book *n*
cook *v*
cook *n*
cough *n*
could (as in past of can
for ability) *v*
country *n*
countryside *n*
cry *v*
cup *n*
curly *adj*

D

dance *n + v*
dangerous *adj*
daughter *n*
dentist *n*
difference *n*
different *adj*
difficult *adj*
doctor *n*
dolphin *n*
down *adv + prep*
downstairs *adv + n*
dream *n + v*
dress up *v*
drive *n*
driver *n*
drop *v*
dry *adj + v*
DVD *n*

E

earache *n*
easy *adj*
e-book *n*
elevator (UK lift) *n*
email *n + v*
every *det*
everyone *pron*
everything *pron*
exciting *adj*
excuse me *dis*

F

fair *adj*
fall *v*
famous *adj*
farm *n*
farmer *n*
fat *adj*
feed *v*
field *n*
film (US movie) *n + v*
film (US movie) *star n*
fine *adj + excl*
first *adj + adv*
fish *v*
fix *v*
floor (e.g. ground, 1st, etc.) *n*
fly *n*
forest *n*
Friday *n*
frightened *adj*
funfair *n*

G

get dressed *v*
get off *v*
get on *v*
get undressed *v*
get up *v*
glass *n*
go shopping *v*
goal *n*
granddaughter *n*
grandparent *n*
grandson *n*
grass *n*
ground *n*
grow *v*
grown-up *n*

H

have (got) to *v*
headache *n*
helmet *n*
help *v*
hide *v*
holiday *n*

homework *n*

hop *v*

hospital *n*

hot *adj*

how *adv*

how much *adv + int*

how often *adv + int*

huge *adj*

hundred *n*

hungry *adj*

hurt *v*

I

ice *n*

ice skates *n*

ice skating *n*

idea *n*

ill *adj*

inside *adv + n + prep*

internet *n*

into *prep*

invite *v*

island *n*

J

jungle *n*

K

kangaroo *n*

kick *n*

kind *n*

kitten *n*

L

lake *n*

laptop *n*

last *adj + adv*

laugh *n + v*

leaf/leaves *n*

library *n*

lift (*US* elevator) *n*

lion *n*

little *adj*

look *for v*

lose *v*

loud *adj*

loudly *adv*

M

machine *n*

map *n*

market *n*

matter *n*

mean *v*

message *n*

milkshake *n*

mistake *n*

model *n*

Monday *n*

moon *n*

more *adv + det + pron*

most *adv + det + pron*

mountain *n*

moustache *n*

move *v*

movie (*UK* film) *n*

must *v*

N

naughty *adj*

near *adv + prep*

neck *n*

need *v*

net *n*

never *adv*

noise *n*

noodles *n*

nothing *pron*

nurse *n*

O

o'clock *adv*

off *adv + prep*

often *adv*

on *adv + prep of time*

only *adv*

opposite *prep*

out *adv*

out *of prep*

outside *adv + n + prep*

P

pair *n*

pancake *n*

panda *n*

parent *n*

parrot *n*

party *n*

pasta *n*

penguin *n*

picnic *n*

pirate *n*

place *n*

plant *n + v*

plate *n*

player *n*

pool *n*

pop *star n*

practice *n*

practise *v*

present *n*

pretty *adj*

puppy *n*

put *on v*

Q

quick *adj*

quickly *adv*

quiet *adj*

quietly *adv*

R

rabbit *n*

rain *n + v*

rainbow *n*

ride *n*

river *n*

road *n*

rock *n*

roller skates *n*

roller skating *n*

roof *n*

round *adj + adv + prep*

S

safe *adj*

sail *n + v*

salad *n*

sandwich *n*

Saturday *n*

sauce *n*

scarf *n*

score *v*

seat *n*

second *adj + adv*

send *v*

shall *v*

shape *n*

shark *n*

shop *v*

shopping *n*

shopping centre
(*US* center) *n*

shoulder *n*

shout *v*

shower *n*

sick *adj*

skate *n + v*

skip *v*

sky *n*

slow *adj*

slowly *adv*

snail *n*

snow *n + v*

someone *pron*

something *pron*

sometimes *adv*

son *n*

soup *n*

sports centre (*US* center) *n*

square *adj + n*

stair(s) *n*

star *n*

station *n*

stomach *n*

stomach-ache *n*

straight *adj*

strong *adj*

Sunday *n*

sunny *adj*

supermarket *n*

surprised *adj*

sweater *n*

sweet *adj*

swim *n*

swimming pool *n*

swimsuit *n*

T

take *v*
take off
(i.e. get undressed) *v*
tall *adj*
tea *n*
teach *v*
temperature *n*
terrible *adj*
text *n + v*
than *conj + prep*
then *adv*
thin *adj*
think *v*
third *adj + adv*
thirsty *adj*
Thursday *n*
ticket *n*
tired *adj*

tooth / teeth *n*
toothache *n*
toothbrush *n*
toothpaste *n*
top *adv + n*
towel *n*
town *n*
town/city *centre*
(*US* center) *n*
tractor *n*
travel *v*
treasure *n*
trip *n*
Tuesday *n*

U

uncle *n*
up *adv + prep*
upstairs *adv + n*

V

vegetable *n*
video *n*
village *n*

W

wait *v*
wake (up) *v*
walk *n*
wash *n + v*
water *v*
waterfall *n*
wave *n*
weak *adj*
weather *n*
website *n*
Wednesday *n*
week *n*
weekend *n*
well *adj + adv*
wet *adj*

whale *n*
when *adv + conj + int*
where *pron*
which *pron*
who *pron*
why *int*
wind *n*
windy *adj*
work *n + v*
world *n*
worse *adj + adv*
worst *adj + adv*
would *v*
wrong *adj*

X

(No words at this level)

Y

yesterday *adv + n*

Z

(No words at this level)

Letters & Numbers

Candidates will be expected to understand and write numbers 21–100 and ordinals 1st to 20th.

Names

Candidates will be expected to recognise and write the following names:

Charlie
Clare
Daisy
Fred
Jack
Jane
Jim
Julia
Lily
Mary
Paul
Peter
Sally
Vicky
Zoe

Appliances

camera
CD (player)
cell phone
clock
computer
cooker
digital camera
DVD (player)
electric
electricity
fridge
gas
heating
lamp
laptop
lights
mobile (phone)
MP3 player
PC
phone
radio
telephone
television / TV
video
washing machine

Clothes and Accessories

bag
bathing suit
belt
blouse
boot
bracelet
cap
chain
clothes
coat
costume (swimming)
dress
earring
fashion
glasses
glove
handbag
hat
jacket
jeans
jewellery / jewelry
jumper
kit
necklace
pocket
purse
raincoat
ring
scarf
shirt
shoes
shorts
skirt
suit
sunglasses
sweater
swimming costume
swimsuit
T-shirt
tie
tights
trainers
trousers
try on v
umbrella
uniform
wallet
watch
wear v

Colours

black
blue
brown
dark
golden
green
grey
light
orange
pale
pink
purple
red
white
yellow

Communication and Technology

address
at / @
by post
call v
camera
CD (player)
cell phone
chat
click v
computer
conversation
digital
digital camera
dot
download n & v
DVD (player)
email n & v
envelope
file
information
internet
keyboard
laptop (computer)
mobile (phone)
mouse
MP3 player
net
online
PC
phone
photograph
photography
printer
screen
software
talk
telephone
text n & v
video
web
web page
website

Documents and Texts

ad / advertisement
article
bill
book
card
comic
diary
diploma
email
form
letter
licence
magazine
menu
message
newspaper
note
notebook
passport
postcard
project
text n & v
textbook
ticket

Education

advanced
beginner
biology
blackboard
board
book
bookshelf
chemistry
class
classmate
classroom
clever
coach
college
course
desk
dictionary
diploma
eraser
exam(ination)
geography
history
homework
information
instructions
know
language
learn
lesson
level
library
mark
maths/mathematics
note
physics
practice n
practise v
project
pupil
read
remember
rubber
ruler
school
science
student
studies
study v
subject
teach
teacher
term
test n
university

Entertainment and Media

act
actor
adventure
advertisement
art
article
board game
book
card

cartoon
CD (player)
chess
cinema
classical (music)
competition
concert
dance n & v
dancer
disco
draw
drawing
drum
DVD (player)
exhibition
festival
film n & v
fun
go out
group
guitar
hip hop
instrument
keyboard
laugh
listen to
look at
magazine
MP3 player
museum
music
musician
news
newspaper
opera
paint v
painter
photograph
photographer
photography
piano
picture
play n
pop (music)
practice n
practise v
programme
project

radio
read v
rock (concert)
screen n
show n
sing
singer
song
television / TV
theatre
ticket
video (game)
watch v

Family and Friends
aunt
boy
brother
child
cousin
dad(dy)
daughter
family
father
friend
friendly
girl
grand(d)ad
grandchild
granddaughter
grandfather
grandma
grandmother
grandpa
grandparent
grandson
granny
group
guest
guy
husband
love n & v
married
Miss
mother
Mr
Mrs
Ms
mum(my)

neighbour
parent
pen-friend
sister
son
surname
teenager
uncle
wife

Food and Drink
apple
bake
banana
barbecue
biscuit
boil
boiled
bottle
bowl
box
bread
break n
breakfast
burger
butter
cafe/café
cafeteria
cake
can n
candy
carrot
cereal
cheese
chef
chicken
chilli
chips
chocolate
coffee
cola
cook n & v
cooker
cream
cup
curry
cut n
dessert
dinner

dish n
drink
eat
egg
fish
food
fork
fridge
fried
fruit
garlic
glass
grape
grilled
honey
hungry
ice
ice cream
jam
juice
kitchen
knife
lemon
lemonade
lunch
main course
meal
meat
melon
menu
milk
mineral water
mushroom
oil
omelette
onion
orange
pasta
pear
pepper
picnic
piece of cake
pizza
plate
potato
rice
roast v & adj
salad

salt
sandwich
sauce
sausage
slice n
snack n
soup
steak
sugar
sweet n & adj
tea
thirsty
toast
tomato
vegetable
waiter
waitress
wash up
yog(h)urt

Health, Medicine and Exercise
accident
ambulance
appointment
arm
baby
back
blood
body
brain
break v
check v
chemist
clean adj & v
cold n
comb n
cut v
danger
dangerous
dead
dentist
die
doctor
Dr
ear
exercise
eye
face

fall *v*
feel *v*
finger
fit
foot
hair
hand
head
health
hear *v*
heart
hospital
hurt *v*
ill
leg
lie down
medicine
neck
nose
nurse
pain
problem
rest *n*
run
sick
soap
stomach
stomach ache
swim
temperature
tired
tooth
toothache
toothbrush
walk
well *adj*

Hobbies and Leisure

barbecue
beach
bicycle
bike
book
camera
camp
camping
campsite
CD (player)
club

collect *v*
computer
dance *n & v*
draw
DVD (player)
festival
go out
guitar
hobby
holidays
join
magazine
member
MP3 player
museum
music
musician
paint *n & v*
park
party
photograph *n & v*
picnic
quiz
tent
video game

House and Home

address
apartment
armchair
bath(tub)
bathroom
bed
bedroom
blanket
bookcase
bookshelf
bowl
box
carpet
chair
clock
computer
cooker
cupboard
curtain
desk
dining room
door

downstairs
drawer
DVD (player)
entrance
flat *n*
floor
fridge
furniture
garage
garden
gas
gate
hall
heating
home
house
key
kitchen
lamp
light
live *v*
living room
pillow
refrigerator
roof
room
safe *adj*
shelf
shower
sink
sitting room
sofa
stay *v*
toilet
towel

Measurements

centimetre /
centimeter
day
degree
gram(me)
half
hour
kilo(gram[me])/kg
kilometre/km/
kilometer
litre / liter
metre / meter

minute
moment
quarter
second
temperature
week
year

Personal Feelings, Opinions and Experiences (adjectives)

able
afraid
alone
amazing
angry
bad
beautiful
better
big
bored
boring
brave
brilliant
busy
careful
clear
clever
cool
different
difficult
excellent
famous
fast
favourite
fine
free
friendly
funny
good
great
happy
hard
heavy
high
hungry
important
interested

interesting
kind
lovely
lucky
married
modern
nice
noisy
old
pleasant
poor
pretty
quick
quiet
ready
real
rich
right
slow
small
soft
sorry
special
strange
strong
sure
sweet
tall
terrible
tired
unhappy
useful
well
worried
wrong
young

Places: Buildings

apartment (building)
bank
block
bookshop
bookstore
building
cafe/café
cafeteria
castle
cinema
college

department store
disco
elevator
entrance
exit
factory
flat
garage
grocery store
guest-house
hospital
hotel
house
library
lift
museum
office
pharmacy
police station
post office
railway station
school
shop
sports centre
stadium
supermarket
swimming pool
theatre
university

Places: Countryside
area
beach
campsite
farm
field
forest
hill
island
lake
mountain
path
railway
rainforest
river
sea
sky
village
wood

Places: Town and City
airport
bridge
bus station
bus stop
car park
city centre
corner
market
motorway
park
petrol station
playground
road
roundabout
square
station
street
town
underground
zoo

Services
bank
cafe / café
cafeteria
cinema
dentist
doctor
garage
hotel
library
museum
petrol station
post office
restaurant
sports centre
swimming pool
theatre
tourist information centre

Shopping
ad / advertisement
assistant
badminton
ball
baseball
basketball

bat
bathing suit
beach
bicycle
bike
bill
boat
bookshop
buy v
cash n & v
catch v
cent
change n & v
cheap
cheque
climb v
close v
closed
club
coach n
competition
cost n & v
credit card
cricket
customer
cycling
department store
dollar
enter (a competition)
euro
expensive
fishing
football
football player
for sale
game
goal
golf
hockey
kit
luck
member
open v & adj
pay (for)
penny
play v
player
pool n

pound
practice n
practise v
price
prize
race n & v
racket
receipt
rent
rest n & v
ride n & v
riding
rugby
run v
sailing
sea
shop
shop assistant
shopper
shopping
skate v
skateboard n
ski v
skiing
snowboard n
snowboarding
soccer
spend
Sport
sport(s)
sports centre
stadium
store
supermarket
surf
surfboard
surfboarding
swim
swimming
swimming costume
swimming pool
swimsuit
table tennis
team
tennis
tennis player
throw v
ticket

tired
trainers
try on
v / versus
volleyball
walk v
watch v
win v
windsurfing
winner

The Natural World
air
autumn
beach
bee
country
countryside
desert
east
explorer
field
fire
flower
forest
grass
grow
hill
hot
ice
island
lake
moon
mountain
north
plant
rabbit
river
sea
sky
south
space
spring
star
summer
tree
water
west
winter

wood
wool
world

Time

a.m./p.m.
afternoon
appointment
autumn
birthday
calendar
century
clock
daily
date
day
diary
evening
half (past)
holidays
hour
January – December
meeting
midnight
minute
moment
Monday – Sunday
month
monthly
morning
night
noon
o'clock
past
quarter (past/to)
second
spring
summer
time
today
tomorrow
tonight
week
weekday
weekend
weekly
winter
working hours
year
yesterday

Travel and Transport

(aero)/(air)plane
airport
ambulance
backpack
boat
bridge
bus
bus station
bus stop
car
case
coach
country
delay n & v
delayed
drive
driver
driving/driver's licence
engine
engineer
explorer
far
flight
fly
garage
helicopter
journey
leave
left
light
luggage
machine
map
mechanic
mirror
miss v
motorbike
motorway
move
oil
park v
passenger
passport
petrol
petrol station
pilot
platform

railway
repair v
return n & v
ride
right
road
roundabout
sailing
seat
ship
station
stop
straight on
street
suitcase
taxi
ticket
tour n
tour guide
tourist
tourist information centre
traffic
traffic light
tram
travel
trip
tyre
underground n
visit
visitor
way n
wheel
window

Weather

cloud
cloudy
cold
fog
foggy
hot
ice
rain
snow
storm
sun
sunny
thunderstorm
warm

weather
wet
wind
windy

Work and Jobs

actor
artist
boss
break n
business
businessman
businesswoman
chemist
cleaner
coach n
company
computer
cook n & v
customer
dentist
desk
diary
diploma
doctor
Dr
driver
earn
email n & v
engineer
explorer
factory
farm
farmer
footballer
football player
guest
guide
instructions
job
journalist
king
letter
manager
mechanic
meeting
message
musician
nurse
occupation

office
painter
photographer
pilot
police officer
queen
receptionist
secretary
shop assistant
shopper
singer
staff
student
teacher
tennis player
tour guide
uniform
waiter/ waitress
work
worker
writer

A1 MOVERS EXAM OVERVIEW

Listening Test

Parts (25 minutes)	What is the skills focus?	What you have to do
1 (5 questions)	Listening for names and descriptions	Draw lines to match names to people in a picture
2 (5 questions)	Listening for names, spellings and other information	Write words or numbers in gaps
3 (5 questions)	Listening for specific information	Match pictures with illustrated items by writing a letter in a box
4 (5 questions)	Listening for specific information	Tick a box under the correct picture
5 (5 questions)	Listening for words, colours and specific information	Colour and write something on the picture

Reading & Writing Test

Parts (30 minutes)	What is the skills focus?	What you have to do
1 (5 questions)	Matching short definitions to words and pictures Writing words	Copy the correct word next to the definition
2 (6 questions)	Reading a dialogue and choosing the correct response	Choose the correct response by circling a letter
3 (6 questions)	Reading for specific information and gist Copying words	Choose and copy missing words correctly Tick a box to choose the correct title for the story
4 (5 questions)	Reading and understanding a factual text Copying words	Complete a text by selecting the correct words and copying them in the gaps
5 (7 questions)	Reading a story Completing sentences	Complete sentences about a story by writing one, two or three words
6 (6 questions)	Writing about a picture	Complete sentences about a picture, answer questions and write two sentences

Speaking Test

Parts (5–7 minutes)	What is the skills focus?	What you have to do
1	Describing two pictures using short responses	Identify four differences between two pictures
2	Understanding the beginning of a story Continuing the story using the picture prompts provided	Describe each picture in turn
3	Suggesting which picture of four is different and saying why	Identify the odd one out and give a reason
4	Understanding and responding to personal questions	Answer personal questions

EXAM OVERVIEW

Cambridge English Qualification A2 Key for Schools Exam, otherwise known as *Cambridge Key for Schools*, is an examination set at A2 level of the Common European Framework of Reference for Languages (CEFR). It is made up of **three papers**, each testing a different area of ability in English: Reading and Writing, Listening, and Speaking.

Reading and Writing	1 hour	50% of the marks
Listening	35 minutes (approximately)	25% of the marks
Speaking	8–10 minutes for each pair of students (approximately)	25% of the marks

All the examination questions are task-based. Rubrics (instructions) are important and candidates should read them carefully. They set the context and give important information about the tasks. There are separate answer sheets for recording answers for the Reading and Writing paper and the Listening paper.

Paper	Format	Task focus
Reading and Writing Seven Parts 32 questions	**Part 1:** three-option multiple choice. Reading six short texts and choosing the correct answer	**Part 1:** reading short texts for the main idea, detail, and writer's purpose.
	Part 2: matching. Reading three short texts or paragraphs on the same topic and matching the correct text or paragraph to the question.	**Part 2:** reading for detailed understanding.
	Part 3: three-option multiple choice. Five multiple-choice questions.	**Part 3:** reading for main idea(s), detail, opinion, attitude and writer's purpose.
	Part 4: three-option multiple-choice cloze. Reading a text with six gaps and selecting the correct word to complete each gap.	**Part 4:** reading and identifying appropriate word.
	Part 5: open cloze. Short text with six gaps. Completing the text with one word in each gap.	**Part 5:** reading and writing appropriate word to fill in the gap.
	Part 6: guided writing; writing a short message. Reading an email or reading about a situation and writing an email.	**Part 6:** Writing an email to a friend including three pieces of information. 25 words or more.
	Part 7: guided writing; writing a short narrative. Three pictures which show a story.	**Part 7:** Writing the short story shown in the three pictures. 35 words or more.
Listening Five Parts 25 questions	**Part 1:** three-option multiple choice. Listening to five short dialogues and choosing the correct picture for each answer.	**Part 1:** listening to identify key information.
	Part 2: gap fill. Listening to a longer monologue and writing the missing word, number, date or time in five gaps.	**Part 2:** listening and writing down information.
	Part 3: three-option multiple choice. Listening to a longer dialogue and choosing the correct answer to five questions.	**Part 3:** listening to identify key information, feelings and opinions.
	Part 4: three-option multiple choice. Listening to five short dialogues or monologues and choosing the correct answer for each text-based question.	**Part 4:** listening for gist, main idea or topic.
	Part 5: matching. Listening to a longer dialogue and matching five questions with seven options. An example is given.	**Part 5:** listening to identify specific information.
Speaking Two Parts	**Part 1:** interview: examiner-led conversation. 3–4 minutes	**Part 1:** giving personal information.
	Part 2: collaborative task: two-way conversation with visual prompt. Examiner asks two more questions to broaden the topic. 5–6 minutes	**Part 2:** asking and answering simple questions, expressing likes and dislikes and giving reasons.